T0182459

An Analysis of

Griselda Pollock's

Vision and Difference: Feminism, Femininity and the Histories of Art

Karina Jakubowicz

Published by Macat International Ltd
24:13 Coda Centre, 189 Munster Road, London SW6 6AW.

Distributed exclusively by Routledge
2 Park Square, Milton Park, Abingdon, Oxon OX14 4RN
711 Third Avenue, New York, NY 10017, USA

Routledge is an imprint of the Taylor & Francis Group, an informa business

www.macat.com
info@macat.com

Cataloguing in Publication Data
A catalogue record for this book is available from the British Library.
Library of Congress Cataloguing-in-Publication Data is available upon request.
Cover illustration: Kim Thompson

ISBN 978-1-912303-94-6 (hardback)
ISBN 978-1-912284-65-8 (paperback)
ISBN 978-1-912284-79-5 (e-book)

Notice
The information in this book is designed to orientate readers of the work under analysis,
to elucidate and contextualise its key ideas and themes, and to aid in the development
of critical thinking skills. It is not meant to be used, nor should it be used, as a
substitute for original thinking or in place of original writing or research. References and
notes are provided for informational purposes and their presence does not constitute
endorsement of the information or opinions therein. This book is presented solely for
educational purposes. It is sold on the understanding that the publisher is not engaged
to provide any scholarly advice. The publisher has made every effort to ensure that
this book is accurate and up-to-date, but makes no warranties or representations with
regard to the completeness or reliability of the information it contains. The information
and the opinions provided herein are not guaranteed or warranted to produce particular
results and may not be suitable for students of every ability. The publisher shall not be
liable for any loss, damage or disruption arising from any errors or omissions, or from
the use of this book, including, but not limited to, special, incidental, consequential or
other damages caused, or alleged to have been caused, directly or indirectly, by the
information contained within.

Printed and bound by CPI Group (UK) Ltd, Croydon, CR0 4YY

CONTENTS

THE MACAT LIBRARY

The Macat Library is a series of unique academic explorations of seminal works in the humanities and social sciences – books and papers that have had a significant and widely recognised impact on their disciplines. It has been created to serve as much more than just a summary of what lies between the covers of a great book. It illuminates and explores the influences on, ideas of, and impact of that book. Our goal is to offer a learning resource that encourages critical thinking and fosters a better, deeper understanding of important ideas.

Each publication is divided into three Sections: Influences, Ideas, and Impact. Each Section has four Modules. These explore every important facet of the work, and the responses to it.

This Section-Module structure makes a Macat Library book easy to use, but it has another important feature. Because each Macat book is written to the same format, it is possible (and encouraged!) to cross-reference multiple Macat books along the same lines of inquiry or research. This allows the reader to open up interesting interdisciplinary pathways.

To further aid your reading, lists of glossary terms and people mentioned are included at the end of this book (these are indicated by an asterisk [*] throughout) – as well as a list of works cited.

Macat has worked with the University of Cambridge to identify the elements of critical thinking and understand the ways in which six different skills combine to enable effective thinking.
Three allow us to fully understand a problem; three more give us the tools to solve it. Together, these six skills make up the **PACIER** model of critical thinking. They are:

ANALYSIS – understanding how an argument is built
EVALUATION – exploring the strengths and weaknesses of an argument
INTERPRETATION – understanding issues of meaning

CREATIVE THINKING – coming up with new ideas and fresh connections
PROBLEM-SOLVING – producing strong solutions
REASONING – creating strong arguments

To find out more, visit **WWW.MACAT.COM.**

CRITICAL THINKING AND *VISION AND DIFFERENCE*

Primary critical thinking skill: INTERPRETATION
Secondary critical thinking skill: CREATIVE THINKING

Vision and Difference encourages readers to interpret visual images in relation to the social, cultural, and political context in which they were produced. It highlights the importance of interpretation, making it clear that interpreting an artwork is a political process that will be affected by our past experiences, value systems, and prejudices. This text illustrates how the reader might clarify the meaning of an artwork using a feminist approach. This style of interpretation considers the lives and experiences of women, and the ways that visual images contribute to the construction of gender.

Griselda Pollock's *Vision and Difference* does not provide an exhaustive study of art history; rather it gives readers the analytical tools to create new connections and readings. Pollock does not restrict her methods to one historical period or artistic medium, instead she gives examples across a broad range of sources, demonstrating how her ideas might be applied to any number of artworks. From Impressionist landscapes to Pre-Raphaelite portraits, photography, advertising, and sculpture, Pollock charts the formation of modern attitudes toward women. Not only does she provide feminist re-readings of works by male artists, such as Degas and Dante Gabriel Rossetti, but she also considers the work of their long-forgotten female contemporaries, such as Mary Cassatt and Berthe Morisot. Both art historians and artists can adopt her theories, and easily create new approaches to the production and analysis of artworks.

ABOUT THE AUTHOR OF THE ORIGINAL WORK

Griselda Pollock (b. 1948) is a renowned critic and art historian. Her feminist approaches to art history have changed the way that images of women are understood and interpreted. Her research champions the work of female artists, and she has written extensively on the work of male artists from a feminist perspective. She is currently Professor of Social and Critical Histories of Art at the University of Leeds.

ABOUT THE AUTHOR OF THE ANALYSIS

Karina Jakubowicz completed her PhD on gardens in the work of Virginia Woolf at University College London. She now teaches at University College London and works with the National Trust. She recently published *Garsington Manor and the Bloomsbury Group* with Cecil Woolf Publishers. Much of her current work focuses on the importance of gardens in the work of early twentieth century writers.

ABOUT MACAT

GREAT WORKS FOR CRITICAL THINKING

Macat is focused on making the ideas of the world's great thinkers accessible and comprehensible to everybody, everywhere, in ways that promote the development of enhanced critical thinking skills.

It works with leading academics from the world's top universities to produce new analyses that focus on the ideas and the impact of the most influential works ever written across a wide variety of academic disciplines. Each of the works that sit at the heart of its growing library is an enduring example of great thinking. But by setting them in context – and looking at the influences that shaped their authors, as well as the responses they provoked – Macat encourages readers to look at these classics and game-changers with fresh eyes. Readers learn to think, engage and challenge their ideas, rather than simply accepting them.

'Macat offers an amazing first-of-its-kind tool for interdisciplinary learning and research. Its focus on works that transformed their disciplines and its rigorous approach, drawing on the world's leading experts and educational institutions, opens up a world-class education to anyone.'

Andreas Schleicher
Director for Education and Skills, Organisation for Economic Co-operation and Development

'Macat is taking on some of the major challenges in university education … They have drawn together a strong team of active academics who are producing teaching materials that are novel in the breadth of their approach.'

Prof Lord Broers,
former Vice-Chancellor of the University of Cambridge

'The Macat vision is exceptionally exciting. It focuses upon new modes of learning which analyse and explain seminal texts which have profoundly influenced world thinking and so social and economic development. It promotes the kind of critical thinking which is essential for any society and economy.
This is the learning of the future.'

Rt Hon Charles Clarke, former UK Secretary of State for Education

'The Macat analyses provide immediate access to the critical conversation surrounding the books that have shaped their respective discipline, which will make them an invaluable resource to all of those, students and teachers, working in the field.'

Professor William Tronzo, University of California at San Diego

WAYS IN TO THE TEXT

KEY POINTS

- Griselda Pollock (b. 1949) is a renowned art historian, artist, and critic.

- Published in 1988, *Vision and Difference* argued that visual images are products of their political context. Pollock stated that art produced by sexist societies often featured and perpetuated patriarchal* ideas.

- *Vision and Difference* is a landmark text that paved the way for a new approach to art history. Pollock made strong connections between certain artworks and the society in which they were produced, and challenged traditional conceptions about what makes an artwork valuable to historians.

Who Is Griselda Pollock?

Griselda Pollock was born in 1949 in Bloemfontein, South Africa, and moved to Canada in 1956. Her family then moved to Britain in 1962, and she attended Queen's College, London, an independent girls' secondary school. In 1967, she went to Oxford University to study Modern History, graduating in 1970. She then attended the Courtauld Institute, University of London, where she completed her MA and PhD. She received her doctorate in 1980 for a study on

Vincent van Gogh* and Dutch art, and she subsequently taught at the universities of Reading and Manchester.

Pollock began to work at the University of Leeds in 1977, and during the 1980s she cemented her reputation as a feminist* and an art critic. She developed her particular approach to art history after becoming increasingly involved in the women's movement.* Art history had long concentrated more or less exclusively on the work of male artists, yet Pollock wrote about the work of female artists, such as Mary Cassatt,* Eva Hesse,* and Charlotte Salomon.* Not only did she emphasize the importance of women in art, she also argued that traditional approaches to art history were inherently sexist* and needed to evolve. She has written several significant texts about women and art, including *Old Mistresses: Women, Art and Ideology** (1981) co-authored with Rozsika Parker, *Differencing the Canon: Feminist Desire and the Writing of Art's Histories*, (1999) and *Dealing with Degas:** Representations of Women and the Politics of Vision* (1992) co-authored with Richard Kendall. She still works at the University of Leeds as Professor of Social and Critical Histories of Art and Director of the Centre for Cultural Studies.* She is a researcher, author, and artist. Her installation *Deadly Tales: A Self-Portrait of a Feminist Intellectual Haunted by Death* was shown at the Leeds Metropolitan Gallery in 1997. Her video art works include *Who is the Other?* (Vancouver Art Gallery, 1993) and *Parallel Lives* (Art Gallery of Western Australia, Perth, 1997).

What Does *Vision And Difference* Say?

Pollock's core argument in *Vision and Difference* is based on the premise that all artworks are a product of their environment. The subject that the artist represents, the way they represent it, their choice of materials, and the resources available to them, are all determined by the time and place in which they work. Consequently, even when an artist is not trying to make a political statement, their work will still be entrenched in the social, cultural, and political context in which it is made. *Vision and Difference* focuses on one aspect of this political environment in particular: the representation of women. Pollock studied the depiction of women in individual artworks, and questioned to what degree these images reinforced sexual inequality.

The core question asked by *Vision and Difference* is: to what extent do systems of representation (namely visual images) feed into the ideology that sustains sexual inequality? Because artworks are a product of their time, they will often reflect on the attitudes toward women during the period in which they were produced. Pollock argued that these artworks will influence the world around them, and may continue to influence people long after the artist is dead. The artwork can thus perpetuate and sustain ideas that may have otherwise become obsolete.

Vision and Difference also examined how women were perceived by art historians, claiming that "the initial task of feminist art history is … a critique of art history itself."[1] Often, art historians viewed women as the subject of artworks, not the creators of them. When women were included in art history books, it was often in the capacity of models, muses, lovers or wives. They were often portrayed as a "passive, beautiful or erotic object[s]," and the concept of creativity was "exclusively tied to the masculine."[2]

Many feminist scholars have called for feminism to be applied to art history, but it was left to researchers such as Pollock to demonstrate how this might work in practice. Her focus on the relationship between systems of representation and ideology created a viable way of doing this. This was what made her different from the other researchers working on the subject at this time. When the text was released, it immediately resonated with a community of feminists and art historians, and its popularity grew over the following years. By 2003, the publisher, Routledge, reprinted the work as part of their "classic" texts series, thus cementing its position as a polemical work.

The argument posited in *Vision and Difference* has a number of implications within the contexts of art history, literature, history, media studies,* and advertising, among other areas. It has meant that more female artists are being studied by art history undergraduates, and that many art history degrees now include courses on feminist art history. While the importance of gender in art history is still not always recognized, Pollock has laid the groundwork for a fairer and more academically rigorous approach to the subject.

Why Does *Vision And Difference* Matter?

Vision and Difference still forms a part of the debate about the place of feminism in the humanities. Pollock argued that gender should not be a subject that is simply tacked on to traditional courses, instead feminism should have an influence on the course as a whole. In her introduction to the Routledge Classics edition of *Vision and Difference*, Pollock points out that "feminist interventions in arts' and cultures' histories are not some nice, optional or avoidable add-on. They are a redefinition of the objects we are studying, and the theories and methods with which we are doing it."[3] Consequently, she believes that feminism should change the overall approach of art history, rather than being consigned to a specific course, or the study of a particular period. As Pollock argued in 2002, the work of feminist theory "has only just begun."[4] She points out that this is the first time in history when there have been enough female professors "to progress an intellectual revolution."[5] She suggests that with more women studying and teaching, there will be a gradual change in what is taught and how.

Outside of academia, *Vision and Difference* can help students to analyze the images that surround them on a daily basis. Using Pollock's ideas, it is possible to see the political subtext that lies behind the portrayal of women in advertising, magazines, and on platforms such as Instagram, Facebook, and online dating agencies. The way that women are depicted and the manner in which they depict themselves, can be seen to be part of a visual "language" that has been sustained over hundreds of years. Fashion models are frequently posed in a way that echoes classical art, with the direction of their gaze and their facial expressions implying passivity or weakness. Women mimic these poses in their online profiles, attempting to look alluring and exhibit their beauty to others. Even the trend for achieving a certain body-type is centered on the notion that women are designed to be looked at.

Several decades after its initial publication, *Vision and Difference* still appears to be a modern text with relevance to contemporary concerns. It is not so out of date that readers have to understand a great deal about the context of its production, or apply it to specific historical circumstances. As feminism becomes an increasingly global movement, texts such as *Vision and Difference* can only gain in importance on a global scale. It is the work of Pollock and her contemporaries that partly forms the bedrock of feminism in its present form.

NOTES

1   Griselda Pollock, *Vision and Difference: Feminism, Femininity and the Histories of Art* (London; New York: Routledge, 2003), 33.

2   Pollock, *Vision and Difference,* 129.

3   Pollock, *Vision and Difference,* xxvii.

4   Pollock, *Vision and Difference,* xxi.

5   Pollock, *Vision and Difference,* xxi.

SECTION 1
INFLUENCES

MODULE 1
THE AUTHOR AND THE
HISTORICAL CONTEXT

KEY POINTS

- *Vision and Difference* is a seminal text in the field of art history.

- Griselda Pollock was an active member of the second-wave feminist movement.*

- Pollock's work was greatly influenced by the feminist movement.

Why Read This Text?

Griselda Pollock's *Vision and Difference* has long been considered a seminal text in the field of art history. It highlights the cultural and political significance of art, and provides a way of finding and interpreting this significance. *Vision and Difference* has had an impact because of its relevance to a broad range of subject areas, and the theories and methods it applies to the processes of representation and interpretation. It is still a highly important text, and continues to increase in importance as Western culture becomes more and more reliant on the use of visual images in order to communicate, advertise, and entertain.

What sets *Vision and Difference* apart from other texts is its unique way of approaching feminist issues through apparently unconnected cultural media. In this work, Pollock was able to argue that the humanities form a major part of contemporary gender politics and have a significant effect on their development. Her importance as a thinker was partly established by this work, and her reputation has continued to grow since the book's publication in 1988. It is partly the

> ❝ This book is a document of my intellectual adventures in that wonderland of radical culture in the 1970s and 1980s. It is informed and transformed by collective work, collaborations, and by encounters with artists, film-makers, and thinkers of all kinds. ❞
>
> Griselda Pollock, *Vision and Difference*, Routledge Classics edition

success of *Vision and Difference* that has caused Pollock to be identified as a key writer on art and cultural history.[1]

Author's Life

Pollock's experience of education had a significant influence on her career, shaping her as an academic and as a feminist. In her contribution to the book *Generations and Geographies in the Visual Arts: Feminist Readings (1996) Pollock described how she* "became involved in feminism slowly and interruptedly" over a number of years, beginning in her early teens.[2] Yet, when she arrived at Oxford University to study Modern History, she found that being highly academic had masculine implications, and began to feel that "intellect and femininity* were not compatible on the scale of social and sexual success."[3] She consequently resisted the label of "feminist" for the majority of her time as an undergraduate. This changed when she studied at the Courtauld Institute of Art, and she realized that her knowledge of art history was chiefly limited to the lives and work of male artists. Furthermore, she understood that this ignorance had been "academically condoned" by lecturers and textbooks that dealt solely with men.[4] Her experience of art history was so male-centric, that she felt the "impossibility, within the existing framework of art history, of imagining women as artists."[5] In other words, the principles that were used to identify and assess artists had been designed around men, and thus precluded or invalidated the work of women. Pollock's perspective on art history meant that her academic efforts were deeply connected with her political ideals, and she began to see art as having a deep and lasting effect on how women are treated and perceived.

Pollock found a group of like-minded thinkers when she joined the London Women's Art History Collective.* The Collective consisted of women who wanted art history to be a part of a wider social and political feminist movement. It emerged out of a public meeting that had been organized in support of the Swedish artist Monica Sjoo,* who was being prosecuted for obscenity after having exhibited her painting *God Giving Birth* in 1971. Griselda Pollock was a founding member of the Collective, and it was through this group that she met Rozsika Parker,* with whom she would later write *Old Mistresses: Women, Art and Ideology*. *Old Mistresses* helped to lay the groundwork for Vision and Difference by arguing for a new approach to art history.

Author's Background

Vision and Difference was a product of the second-wave feminist movement, of which Pollock was an active member. This women's liberation movement extended roughly from the 1960s to the 1980s and, as with the first wave* of this movement, it was primarily concerned with obtaining equal rights for women. A distinctive element of the second-wave movement was that culture and politics were seen as being inextricably linked, and feminists exposed sexism* in the media and in academia, as well as protesting its existence in the government and the workplace. Pollock's work was in tune with this mindset, since it made a clear case for art being deeply connected with the realities of everyday life and politics at the highest level. Pollock's ability to link art history with contemporary politics, was aided by the number of female artists producing overtly feminist art in the 1960s and 1970s. That these women used art as a way to express their frustrations and ideas, proved that art could be a radical and vital aspect of the women's movement and of politics as a whole.

Pollock's work would have been very different (if not impossible) without the academic and political feminist communities of which she was a part. As she wrote in the first chapter of the book, "[no] doubt the focus of my concerns is conditioned by the conversational community within which I work and to which I have access through the magazines, conferences, exhibitions and educational institutions."[6] Being an educated woman working in academia, meant she saw how feminism was being applied to academic subjects, such as history, literature, media studies, and psychology.* She claims that the "massive expansion of feminist studies attendant on the resurgence of the women's movement in the late 1960s" was "critical" to her work.[7] The feminist movement was reshaping the intellectual landscape, and providing new methods for academic enquiry.

NOTES

1   Chris Murray, ed. *Key Writers on Art: The Twentieth Century* (London: Routledge, 2003).

2   Griselda Pollock, ed., *Generations and Geographies in the Visual Arts: Feminist Readings (London: Routledge, 1996), 12.*

3   Pollock, ed., *Generations and Geographies*, 12.

4   Pollock, *Generations and Geographies*, 13.

5   Pollock, *Generations and Geographies*, 13.

6   Griselda Pollock, *Vision and Difference: Feminism, Femininity and the Histories of Art* (London; New York: Routledge, 2003), 21.

7   Pollock, *Vision and Difference*,10.

MODULE 2
ACADEMIC CONTEXT

KEY POINTS

- Griselda Pollock felt that the practice of art history needed to fundamentally change.
- At the time when she was writing *Vision and Difference*, feminist art historians were chiefly concerned with issues of representation and history.
- Pollock was influenced by thinkers both within and beyond feminist theory.

The Work In Its Context

When Griselda Pollock started writing *Vision and Difference*, she felt that approaches to art history needed to drastically change. In her opinion, it was not enough to simply put women artists on the syllabus, she felt that the whole of art history was a "masculinist discourse."[1] In other words, she felt that art history revolved around the work and opinions of men. This position was far from unfounded, since the subject focused chiefly on male artists, and the use of critical theory (let alone feminist theory) was limited. Pollock's introduction to *Vision and Difference* attests to the inequality at the time when she was writing. As an example, she describes the four-year degree course that she was teaching at Leeds, and states that while her students did study feminist approaches to art, they did so for only twenty weeks.[2] She added that despite this rather paltry amount, an external assessor suggested that there might be "too much feminism" on the course.[3]

Art history was not the only discipline that was adapting to the addition of feminist approaches, and the inclusion of female figures and perspectives. The study of literature was being revolutionized by

> **❝ Art history is not just indifferent to women; it is a masculinist discourse, party to the social construction of sexual difference. ❞**
> Griselda Pollock, *Vision and Difference*, Routledge Classics edition

the inclusion and discovery of female writers who had previously been ignored. Furthermore, feminist approaches to literature were uncovering how the experiences of women were documented in fiction. Not every institution or discipline was eager to change, but across the arts and humanities there were many academics who were adapting their courses to facilitate feminist discourse.

Overview Of The Field

At the time when Pollock was writing *Vision and Difference*, work on feminism and art typically divided into two camps, these can be broadly grouped as studies of representation and studies of history.

Studies of representation were concerned with the way that women were depicted in art, and with the dynamics of who was viewing whom and how. John Berger* was one of the key participants in this discussion. His book, *Ways of Seeing* (1972) was based on a British Broadcasting Corporation (BBC) television series of the same name, and it demonstrated that visual images had hidden meanings that were bound up in the ideologies that the artist was exposed to. He also emphasized that throughout history, women have been depicted in art as being looked at, while men have been portrayed as the ones looking. He argues that this sets up a power dynamic that almost always places men in a position of dominance. Berger links the power relations signified in art to a wider social environment. He wrote that a woman has to "survey everything she is and everything she does because how she appears to others, and ultimately how she appears to men, is of crucial importance for what is normally thought of as the success of her life."[4]

Jaqueline Rose* was also concerned with how art represented women, and she was particularly interested in the ideologies that are consciously or unconsciously communicated in images. Her book *Sexuality in the Field of Vision* (1986) explored several of the themes that arise in *Vision and Difference,* such as feminism, psychoanalysis, semiotics,* and film theory. In *Sexuality in the Field of Vision,* Rose considered how sexuality was constructed through visual symbols and signs.

Certain thinkers were particularly concerned with feminist *histories* of art rather than the production of art itself. They were interested in exposing women artists that had been forgotten or overlooked, but moreover they wanted to change the way art history was studied so that it might be more applicable to women. Linda Nochlin's* 1971 article "Why Have There Been No Great Women Artists?" was a groundbreaking text in this regard. In this article, she suggested that the criterion of "greatness" had been defined by men, leaving women excluded by its very nature. Nochlin's article stated that inequality was not simply created by law or regulations, but also generated by the very systems and languages that humans have developed in order to interpret the world. The study of art history was a part of this system, and in Nochlin's mind it not only ignored women, it also reinforced inequality.[5]

Academic Influences

Prior to the publication of *Vision and Difference,* there were several writers who had explored many of the major themes in Pollock's work, including the concepts of feminist art history and of "vision" or seeing. Nochlin, Berger, and Rose all influenced Pollock and helped lay the groundwork for both *Vision and Difference,* and Pollock's earlier texts *Old Mistresses* (1986) and *Framing Feminism* (1987). *Framing Feminism* is a collection of essays on feminism and art that Pollock edited with Rozsika Parker, and it includes a number of voices that undoubtedly influenced Pollock while she was writing *Vision and*

21

Difference. The book included writers such as Laura Mulvey,* Mary Kelly,* and Parker. Mulvey's work dealt with the representation of women in art and cinema, and often demonstrated a psychoanalytical approach to feminism. Parker's work was closely aligned with Pollock's, but in *Framing Feminism* her articles dealt mainly with the history of the women's movement in the art community. Kelly is an artist and academic who focused on the relationship between feminism and contemporary art. Her 1986 article, "Desiring Images/Imaging Desire," explored the role of desire in the way viewers relate to images.

Pollock had also been inspired by the work and methods of several thinkers outside of feminism and the art world. The most important influences on her work were undoubtedly Karl Marx,* Michel Foucault,* and Sigmund Freud,* all of whom she cited at the start of *Vision and Difference.* Their work offered methods that Pollock was able to use in order to describe and penetrate the ideology of patriarchal society and the production of knowledge.* Marx argued that cultural ideology expressed and sustained certain power relations, and he also referred to the production of these meanings within the context of political structures.[6] While Pollock admitted that Marx was not a feminist, she stated that it is "important to take advantage of the theoretical and historiographical revolution which the Marxist tradition represents."[7] Foucault also studied the production of ideology, but focused more specifically on the history of sexuality. He also posited that sexuality first gained ideological significance among the middle classes, and considered sexuality in relation to gender and class.[8]

Freud's work on psychoanalysis was important to Pollock, since she felt it was an essential part of understanding why patriarchal* societies develop in the first place. Paraphrasing Juliet Mitchell* in her work *Psychoanalysis and Feminism*, Pollock wrote that "Freudian* theory offers not a prescription for a patriarchal society but a description of one which we can use to understand its functionings."[9]

Pollock's use of Freudian psychoanalysis is designed to explain how ideology functions (why men are driven to represent women in a certain way, for example), while her use of Marx and Foucault explains the historical and economic situation surrounding the artist.[10]

NOTES

1   Griselda Pollock, *Vision and Difference: Feminism, Femininity and the Histories of Art* (London; New York: Routledge, 2003), 15.

2   Pollock, *Vision and Difference*, 12.

3   Pollock, *Vision and Difference*, 12.

4   Pollock, *Vision and Difference*, 49.

5   Linda Nochlin, *The Feminism and Visual Culture Reader*, "Why Have There Been no Great Women Artists?" 231.

6   Karl Marx, *Grundrisse: A Contribution to the Critique of Political Economy*, (London: Penguin, 1993).

7   Pollock, *Vision and Difference*, 7.

8   Michel Foucault, *History of Sexuality Volume I: The Will to Knowledge* (London: Penguin, 1998).

9   Pollock, *Vision and Difference*, 17.

10 Pollock, *Vision and Difference*, 3–4, 15.

MODULE 3
THE PROBLEM

KEY POINTS

- Academics were still unsure about how to incorporate feminism into art history.

- Many feminists felt that art history needed to change, but they differed in regard to how it might change.

- Griselda Pollock wanted to deconstruct both art and the histories written about it, and to analyze it on a structural level.

Core Question

The core question of Griselda Pollock's *Vision and Difference*, what Linda Nochlin calls the "woman question,"[1] can be simply phrased as, "How do we incorporate women and feminism into academic debate, and what implications does this have for feminism more broadly?"

The lives and perspectives of women had long been absent from academic discourse, and thinkers differed in terms of how exactly to include these new and challenging elements. It was accepted that the way feminism was treated by art historians would have far-reaching implications, yet a specific method or approach had not been developed. Many texts—including Jacqueline Rose's *Sexuality in the Field of Vision*, and John Berger's *Ways of Seeing*—had only just begun to decode the facts of sexual inequality, and fell short of suggesting a theoretical framework within which to manage this process. For the most part, a framework was developed by academics simply producing research that concerned female artists or feminism and art. As they did so, it was possible to see how different thinkers had different approaches, and that these approaches produced conclusions that varied in their

> ❝ The so-called woman question, far from being a minor, peripheral, and laughably provincial sub-issue grafted onto a serious, established discipline, can become a catalyst, an intellectual instrument, probing basic and 'natural' assumptions, providing a paradigm* for other kinds of internal questioning. ❞
>
> Linda Nochlin, "Why Have There Been No Great Women Artists?"

insightfulness and value. In this way, a whole community of academics gradually developed methods and ideas that are still used today.

The Participants

As art historians started to incorporate feminism into their work, different trends and opinions emerged. Some thinkers simply turned their attention to female artists, studying them in much the same manner as they would male artists, while others focused on the practical and social barriers that prevented women from being artists. Germaine Greer's book on feminism and art, *The Obstacle Race* (1979), is a combination of these two methodologies. The text exposed a number of neglected artists, while describing the difficulties that women faced throughout history in their bid to create art and to be recognized as artists. Greer's status as a famous feminist helped to bring the issue of women artists more fully into the popular consciousness.

Many other art historians felt that the subject of art history needed to fundamentally change. Norma Broude* and Mary Garrard* had called for a revision of the very idea of art history, suggesting the "possibility of *alterations* of art history itself, its methodology and its theory."[2] Linda Nochlin also called for feminism to bring about a paradigm shift within the subject, stating that a feminist critique of the discipline of art history is needed "that can pierce cultural-ideological limitations," and "reveal biases and inadequacies … of the discipline as a whole."[3] The art historian T. J. Clark* also argued for a fundamental shift, and for what he called a "social history of art."[4] In Clark's opinion, this would not simply be a "cheerful diversification of the subject," but a "disintegration" of it; a breaking down of traditional methodological approaches.[5]

The Contemporary Debate

Many of Griselda Pollock's key ideas, including her argument that feminist art history was a political as well as an academic undertaking, had appeared in the text Pollock had previously written with Rozsika Parker, *Old Mistresses: Women, Art and Ideology*, which also put forward the notion that feminist art history was an analysis of art history in itself, and of the sociological factors, language, and culture that are relevant to it. Pollock was also influenced by her collaboration with Deborah Cherry,* and one of the chapters in *Vision and Difference* ("Woman as Sign in Pre-Raphaelite* Literature: The Representation of Elizabeth Siddall"*) was co-written with Cherry.

Works such as Greer's *Obstacle Race* did not go far enough, in Pollock's opinion, toward a more equal academic discourse. In *Vision and Difference*, Pollock set her work apart from that of Greer. Quoting a review of the text by Rozsika Parker, she wrote: "It is not the obstacles that Germaine Greer cites that really count, but the rules of the game which demand scrutiny."[6] Pollock did not want to produce another history of women's struggle; instead, her aim was to penetrate the social and psychological structures that underpinned that struggle. In this assertion Pollock was greatly indebted to Nochlin, whose article "Why Have There Been No Great Women Artists?" laid the groundwork for Pollock's approach to feminist art history. Pollock ultimately disagrees with some of Nochlin's conclusions, and in particular with her desire to dispel patriarchal ideologies, but not to examine them. Nonetheless, Nochlin's call for a revised understanding of "greatness" comes very close to the premise of *Vision and Difference*.[7]

Pollock was also indebted to Clark who, like Pollock, used a Marxist approach in his critique of art. However, while she agreed that the "paradigm for the social history of art lies within Marxist cultural theory and historical practice," she disagreed with his lack of attention to sexual difference.[8] She argued that "as much as society is structured by relations of inequality at the point of material production, so too is it structured by sexual divisions and inequalities."[9]

NOTES

1   Linda Nochlin, "Why Have There Been No Great Women Artists?" *ARTnews* (January 1971) reprinted in *The Feminism and Visual Culture Reader,* 2nd ed. (London: Routledge, 2003), 263.

2   Norma Broude and Mary D. Garrard, eds., *Feminism and Art History: Questioning the Litany* (New York: Harper & Row 1982), vii.

3   Linda Nochlin, "Why Have There Been No Great Women Artists?" 263.

4   Timothy James Clark, "On the Conditions of Artistic Creation," *Times Literary Supplement*, May 24, 1974, 562.

5   Clark, "On the Conditions of Artistic Creation," 562.

6   Griselda Pollock, *Vision and Difference: Feminism, Femininity and the Histories of Art* (London; New York: Routledge, 2003), 33.

7   Pollock, *Vision and Difference*, 48–50.

8   Pollock, *Vision and Difference*, 27.

9   Pollock, *Vision and Difference*, 27.

MODULE 4
THE AUTHOR'S CONTRIBUTION

KEY POINTS

- *Vision and Difference* was one of the strongest examples of feminist art criticism published at the time.
- Griselda Pollock's approach involved decoding images and studying their social and political context.
- The text ought to be considered in the wider context of feminist art history.

Author's Aims

In 1988, the core subjects in Griselda Pollock's *Vision and Difference*, namely those of feminism, femininity, and art history, were not at all revolutionary. In some ways, her work was the sum of a collective movement toward a feminist art history. Certain methods and ideas in her work had been used before, but not all of them had been combined in the same text, or applied in the way she applied them. *Vision and Difference* was one of the first book-length examples of feminist art criticism, and the range of her methods and subjects showed the breadth of its forms and applications. It worked on two levels, examining both the representation of women in works of art, and the representation of the work of art within the context of art history. In this way, she was able to consider the artist and the art historian side by side, and demonstrate that they are both responsible for creating reflections of the world around them.

While most of *Vision and Difference* built on work carried out previously by Pollock and others, the text did have elements that were fairly new. The chapter on "Modernity and the Spaces of Femininity" began to explore how women were presented in relation to the space

> 66 The essays collected [in *Vision and Difference*] represent a contribution to a diversified and heterogeneous range of practices which constitute the feminist intervention in art history. 99
>
> Griselda Pollock, *Vision and Difference*, Routledge Classics edition

around them. It also considered the role of women as viewers in the gallery space, a concept that Pollock built upon in her later work *Encounters in the Virtual Feminist Museum* (2007).

The work covered a broad range of ideas, and Pollock herself refers to it as "a series of interlinked case studies."[1] Yet all of the individual ideas in *Vision and Difference* contribute to the overarching argument that ideology and the notion of "difference" is partly sustained and expounded through the use of created images, such as paintings, photographs, and films. Pollock's particular methods, namely her use of Freud and Marx, have had a profound impact on contemporary art history and gender studies.* While Pollock's method focuses on art specifically, it also provides students with the tools they need to read any image of or by a woman. For example, the portrayal of women in advertising, fashion, and pornography is now an important part of the third-wave feminist movement,* and the ways in which these images are read are typically influenced by the methods that Pollock advocated.

It is difficult to trace the impact made specifically by *Vision and Difference*, since it was one of a group of texts that argued for feminist interventions in art history. Combined with these other texts it contributed enormously to the understanding of feminism in an academic context, and put pressure on academic institutions to include feminism in their teaching of certain subjects. Pollock's argument was that the politics of gender permeated academia on every level, from the methods of enquiry to the design of the courses and the subjects studied. This compelled students and teachers to re-evaluate the relationship between high culture and contemporary politics.

Vision and Difference can be described as a "game-changer," since it made feminist art history an issue for feminists and art historians more generally. It also provided a method for feminist art historians that was workable, and suggested theories and readings that might be used in order to tackle what had been a highly neglected subject.

Approach

Pollock's approach was connected with her belief that the paradigm of art history needed to be altered. Her approach was centered on examining the ideologies that underpinned the practice of art history. Using the methods of Foucault and Marx, while also adopting semiotics and psychoanalytic theory in places, Pollock was able to decode visual images and the circumstances around their production. The fact that she took the social and political context of the work into account, meant that she was able to produce readings that explored the social and gender inequalities implicit in these works. Whereas a traditional art historian may have focused more on compositional structure, medium, and style, Pollock was particularly interested in what was being represented and how. In her chapter on the spaces of femininity, for example, she considers the spaces in which women were depicted in Impressionist* art, and demonstrates how this connects to the position of women in society at the time. Using art by and about women, Pollock found clues that revealed the realities of their lives.

Like so many other academics, Pollock was addressing the "woman question," and attempting to find successful ways of incorporating feminism into analytical practice. What set Pollock apart was her range of methods, ideas, and subjects. *Vision and Difference* represented a broad and dynamic study of women and art that was at once ambitious and effective.

Contribution In Context

Vision and Difference was very much a product of its contemporary cultural and intellectual environment. Pollock's work would have been impossible without the political and academic feminist communities in which she played such an active role. As she writes in *Vision and Difference*, feminist art history "is ultimately defined within that collective critique of social, economic and ideological power which is the women's movement."[2] Consequently, she was inspired by feminist theorists working in a number of disciplines, by contemporary feminist artists, and not least of all by the women's movement in general. More specifically, Pollock's work was rooted in the research of other feminist art historians, and it made for a strong continuation of previous ideas. The key difference between *Vision and Difference* and previous publications was the length of the text, and the detailed and varied application of ideas. While *Vision and Difference* was original in parts, it also expanded on pre-existing work by Pollock and others, thus creating an epitome of feminist art criticism at the period. The work included and reinforced some of the most persuasive ideas coming from feminist art historians at the time, creating a strong and representative case for feminist art history in general.

NOTES

1 Griselda Pollock, *Vision and Difference: Feminism, Femininity and the Histories of Art* (London; New York: Routledge, 2003), xxxiv.

2 Pollock, *Vision and Difference*, 24.

SECTION 2
IDEAS

MODULE 5
MAIN IDEAS

KEY POINTS

* The key themes of the text are the representation of women, the construction of femininity, and the history of art.
* Griselda Pollock argues that works of art will reflect of the social and political environment in which they are made.
* She expresses herself using academic language and ideas.

Key Themes

The main themes of Griselda Pollock's *Vision and Difference* are indicated in the subtitle of the text: *Feminism, Femininity and the Histories of Art*. The terms used in the subtitle highlight the text's core concerns, the first being a political movement (feminism), the second a psychoanalytical term for a position within the structure of sexual difference (femininity), and the third being histories of art. The terms "vision" and "difference" describe the angle taken in considering these themes. "Vision" illustrates the importance of sight and perspective, of how looking is done and by whom. The "difference" alluded to is that of the sexual and social difference that Pollock believes is partly facilitated and demonstrated through images. These themes emerge as the text develops, and are treated concurrently.

The first chapter of the text ("Feminist Interventions in the Histories of Art") examines the need for feminism in art history, and asks what the addition of feminism to art history entails for the researcher. It also outlines Pollock's basic theoretical approach. The second chapter ("Vision, Voice and Power: Feminist Art Histories and Marxism"*) shows how the production of artistic images is embedded

> **❝** Art history itself is to be understood as a series
> of representational practices which actively produce
> definitions of sexual difference and contribute to the
> present configuration of sexual politics and power
> relations. **❞**
>
> Griselda Pollock, *Vision and Difference,* Routledge Classics edition

in power relationships, and consequently perpetuates the structures of
power within society. The title of this chapter shows how deeply
Pollock's analysis is indebted to the theories of Karl Marx. Her next
chapter ("Modernity and the Spaces of Femininity") highlights where
and how female subjects are located in artworks. It focuses on the
portrayal of modernity in French Impressionism, comparing the way
that a male artist, such as Edouard Manet,* presented women and
how female artists, such as Mary Cassatt* and Berthe Morisot, did. In
Chapter Four ("Woman as Sign"), Pollock focuses specifically on the
Pre-Raphaelites. She considers how members of the Pre-Raphaelite
Brotherhood portrayed women, using the case of Elizabeth Siddall as a
key example. She also argues that many art historians have perpetuated
the idea of Siddall as created by the Brotherhood, instead of exercising
an objective perspective of her character. This chapter demonstrates
Pollock's themes extremely well. Siddall was both an artist and an
artist's model, and this enabled Pollock to approach the themes of
visual representation alongside the treatment of women artists by art
historians. Her photo essay, which follows this chapter, encourages the
reader to draw comparisons between modern images and those
generated by the Pre-Raphaelites. In Chapter Six ("Woman as Sign:
Psychoanalytical Readings"), Pollock considers why women are
portrayed in particular ways, and uses a psychological perspective to
explore this issue. Having demonstrated her key themes in varying
levels of detail, Pollock then applies these ideas to a more modern

context in "Screening the Seventies." In this, her final chapter, Pollock explores a range of installations, photographs, and advertisements, demonstrating how her ideas can be applied to a broad range of images and media.

The themes fit together to produce Pollock's overarching argument that sexual difference is constructed through and alongside vision (both what we look at and how). This plays a role in the construction of femininity, which is partially defined by visual image and how the way in which we look and what we look at is represented in these images. The ultimate conclusion is that histories of art, being a study of visual images, are innately involved in the project of feminism.

Exploring The Ideas

The predominant idea that Pollock proposed in *Vision and Difference* is that artistic representations of women are products of the artist's social and political environment. In sexist societies, women are typically depicted in a way that indicates their oppression. Even if an artist is not particularly sexist, they will portray the ideologies around them by virtue of representing the world around them. By looking closely at the images that these artists create, it is possible to see complex and fascinating ideological concepts at work. The way the female body is presented, how it is dressed, the characters that the models depict, and the way the figure is presented in relation to the space around them, are all indications of a wider context.

Underpinning Pollock's main idea, is that our interpretation of works of art will also be a product of our social and political surroundings. If the dominant ideology is formed by men for the benefit of men, then both the art that is produced and the way that art is viewed, will predominantly speak to patriarchal interests. Pollock argues that art history has been a patriarchal discourse, and it has been chiefly interested in art by men. She emphasizes that writing history (like creating art) is always a political process that will be affected by the writer's environment. She explains that there are many different "histories" of art, and that "art history has a history."[1]

Pollock's work goes further by explaining that if histories of art are inherently sexist, they will then reinforce sexism. By focusing only on male artists, and by failing to address the fundamental ideologies behind artworks, art historians can become complicit in oppression. She writes that "women have not been omitted [from art history] through forgetfulness or mere prejudice. The structural sexism of most academic disciplines contributes actively to the production and perpetuation of a gender hierarchy."[2] She felt that it was the role of art historians to decode and explore ideology, rather than strengthen it. She states that, "not only do we have to grasp that art is a part of social production, but we also have to realize that it is itself productive, that is, it actively produces meanings."[3]

Language And Expression

As an ambitious and often complex text, *Vision and Difference* can be a challenging book for students to read. It was intended for fellow academics and students working in the humanities, and thus relies on the reader having some background knowledge of the subject. Terms such as feminism, ideology, and patriarchy are crucial to the meaning of the work, and if the reader is not familiar with them then the text might be very awkward to negotiate. The breadth of Pollock's research can also be problematic, since she jumps between several difficult questions and ideas, while using wide ranging examples from various periods. Once the reader has grasped the ideas underpinning one chapter, they then must move on to another subject and begin again. For a student who is familiar with feminist art history this can make for an invigorating and stimulating experience, but it might be tedious for those who are just beginning to understand the basics. Pollock's ambitious subject matter, her use of theory, and what has been called her "awkwardness of language," can make *Vision and Difference* slightly difficult for some.[4]

NOTES

1   Griselda Pollock, *Vision and Difference: Feminism, Femininity and the Histories of Art* (London; New York: Routledge, 2003), xxiv.

2   Pollock, *Vision and Difference*, 1.

3   Pollock, *Vision and Difference*, 42.

4   Carol Zemel, "Review of *Vision and Difference*," *The Art Bulletin* 72.2 (June 1990): 336–41.

MODULE 6
SECONDARY IDEAS

KEY POINTS

- Griselda Pollock explores the representation of women as signs that carry ideological meaning.
- She argues that these signs signify order and sexual difference.
- While the key elements of her argument have been influential, details of her work have been ignored.

Other Ideas

A significant secondary theme in Griselda Pollock's *Vision and Difference* is the concept of "woman as sign." This phrase was developed by Elizabeth Cowie* in her article of the same name in the feminist magazine *m/f*.[1] It emphasized the importance of signifying systems in the production of gender difference, and suggested that images of women were often signs and symbols for a variety of social meanings, instead of being artistic representations of a human being. Pollock expands on this notion using works by Pre-Raphaelite artists, and argues that their images of women are often signifying femaleness, rather than attempting to represent an actual woman. Focusing in particular on paintings by Dante Gabriel Rossetti,* Pollock shows that while the images may look realistic, they are in fact anatomically incorrect. She shows that the hairline of the model is often drawn down, the forehead reduced, and the eyes placed high up on the head. She argues that the artist was not interested in depicting a real woman with typical facial proportions, instead they were using the woman's face as a signifier of femininity.

> **❝ The practice of painting is itself a site for the inscription of sexual difference. ❞**
> Griselda Pollock, *Vision and Difference*, Routledge Classics edition

Pollock takes the Pre-Raphaelite model Elizabeth Siddall as a key example. While giving a detailed biography of Siddall, Pollock proves that both artists and art historians misrepresented her. She points out that Siddall was persistently given the wrong name by both contemporaries and art historians. While the artists who painted her preferred to use nicknames or altered spellings, art historians were similarly lax, opting for "Lizzy" or "Lizzie" instead of Elizabeth, and spelling her second name "Siddal." Pollock argued that the disregard for Siddall's actual name proves that she was treated as a signifier by previous and contemporary art historians. She writes that "'Siddal' functions as a sign. More than the name of an historical personage it does not simply refer to a woman, or even Woman."[2] She concluded that for both the artists and art historians, the model known as "Siddal" was simply a sign for masculine creativity.

Exploring The Ideas

Pollock's argument that women in art are used as symbols relates to her overarching claim that paintings use a visual language (semiotics) in order to express complex ideological ideas. She describes a signifying practice as "an organization of elements which *produce* meanings, construct images of the world, and strive to fix certain meanings, to effect particular ideological representations of the world."[3] Various signifiers in a painting include: the depiction of the figure, their positioning, their face, the environment they are depicted in, their clothes (or lack thereof), the viewer of the painting, and the context in which the painting is displayed—to name but a few. Through these symbolic systems, the paintings sustain the ideologies of a particular society. Pollock goes further to explain that these images are a part of maintaining social order. She writes that, "woman as a sign signifies social order; if the sign is misused it can threaten disorder."[4] In other words, a painting of a woman that is in keeping with ideology will be considered socially acceptable, whereas as a painting that depicts a woman in an unconventional or rebellious way, is seen as a threat to social order.

Part of the power relations encoded in a work of art, is the politics of who is looking at whom. Throughout history, women have been depicted by men in art, and their images are then looked at by men in galleries. Typically, these women are posed in such a way that their eyes are averted from the viewer: they do not look back. As Pollock writes, "like the goddesses of the Hollywood screen they take on an iconic fascination of being seen, while *unseeing*."[5] She argues that it is through these power dynamics and the visual symbolism of the painting, that the artist is able to depict sexual difference. This "difference" is not the basic anatomical difference between the male and female body, rather it a whole set of ideas and symbols that are woven around the concepts of "male" and "female," and which sets them in opposition. Through encoding "the social construction of sexual difference," art contributes to our definition of what it means to be a man or a woman.[6]

Overlooked

Many of Pollock's smaller points in *Vision and Difference* have not received much attention, but this is partly due to the context in which the book is typically read. As "a foundational text," for students becoming familiar with feminist art history, it tends to be read for its general approach to visual images and gender difference.[7] The last chapter of the book ("Screening the Seventies") also receives far less attention than the rest of the work because it is less coherent, and shifts the focus awkwardly from painted matter to film and photography.

Pollock's work on Elizabeth Siddall has received attention in light of Pollock's argument that women are used as signifiers. However, the points that she makes about the representation of Siddall have mostly fallen on deaf ears. She is still romanticized or framed as a tragic figure, and her name is still misspelled, even by her own biographers.[8] As Pollock writes, she often wonders "why subsequent books on Elizabeth Siddall and Dante Gabriel Rossetti have never felt it necessary to acknowledge fully the arguments Deborah Cherry and I put forward about the historical person of Elizabeth Siddall."[9]

Vision and Difference is ripe for reconsideration, and will benefit from being read in different contexts. It is just acquiring the status of a "classic" work, and is already beginning to typify a particular phase in feminism and art history. This means that chapters such as "Screening the Seventies" can be seen as historical and social documents, and used to shed light on feminism in the 1970s and 1980s. It is also possible for readers to apply Pollock's methods to more recent forms of representation, such as the images of women on the Internet or in video games.

NOTES

1   Elizabeth Cowie, "Woman as Sign" *m/f* 1.1 (1978), 50.

2   Griselda Pollock, *Vision and Difference: Feminism, Femininity and the Histories of Art* (London; New York: Routledge, 2003), 134.

3   Pollock, *Vision and Difference*, 43.

4   Pollock, *Vision and Difference*, 45.

5   Pollock, *Vision and Difference*, 210.

6   Pollock, *Vision and Difference*, 12.

7   Grant Pooke and Diana Newall, *Art History: The Basics* (London: Routledge, 2008), 162.

8   Lucinda Hawksley, *Lizzie Siddal: Face of the Pre-Raphaelites* (New York: Walker, 2006).

9   Pollock, *Vision and Difference*, xxxvii.

MODULE 7
ACHIEVEMENT

KEY POINTS

- *Vision and Difference* demonstrates how feminist theory might be applied to art history in a number of ways. It uses a broad range of artworks from a number of periods.

- The text is highly relevant outside of art history.

- Its relevance is somewhat limited to a middle-class, Western experience of gender and art.

Assessing The Argument

Griselda Pollock's *Vision and Difference* succeeded in making a strong case for a feminist art history, and it gave a clear overview of what feminist art criticism looked like in practice. The book developed those theories put forward *Old Mistresses: Women, Art and Ideology*, the book that Pollock co-wrote with Rozsika Parker. In this text, they argued that to write art history should be to "expose its underlying values, its assumptions, its silences and its prejudices."[1] *Vision and Difference* not only proposes this same argument, it also gives detailed and extensive examples of how to carry out such a project. For example, the second chapter ("Vision, Voice and Power") explores the methods that might underpin a feminist art history. It considers how Marxism might aid the analysis of art, and studies the approaches of thinkers such as Linda Nochlin and Kate Millett.* Having presented a number of approaches, the following chapter ("Modernity and the Spaces of Femininity") then demonstrates a feminist reading of art history. The chapter focuses on a particular artistic movement (Impressionism) and on a particular aspect of women's experience (their relationship with and access to physical space).

❝ An audacious and thrilling call to arms. ❞
Carol Zemel, review of Vision and Difference, The Art Bulletin, Vol. 72

While the book suffers from a lack of specific focus, it also gives a good indication of how broadly, and in what ways, feminist theory can be applied to art criticism. By considering works that were produced at different historical periods, Pollock is able to show how these works were affected by their respective social context.

Achievement In Context

Vision and Difference has had an unexpected relevance to subjects outside of art history, such as literature and media studies. It has now become a key text for students of gender studies, media, literature, and film. Pollock could not have known to what degree her work would apply to other subjects, but the potential for inter-disciplinarity was innate to the text's themes and ideas. She wrote in *Vision and Difference* that "Feminist interventions in arts' and cultures' histories are not some nice, optional or avoidable add-on. They are a redefinition of the objects we are studying, and the theories and methods with which we are doing it."[2] To do this meant investigating other modes of representation, such as writing, spoken language, advertising, photography, and film. Consequently, her book attracted interest from other researchers in sociology,* literary studies, psychology, and history, as well as from her initial target audience.

The ideas underlying *Vision and Difference* have been successfully adapted to the study of literature, film, and culture in particular. Pollock's understanding of the "male gaze" and of female representation have been applied to literary studies, such as *Textual Intersections* (2009) edited by Rachael Langford, and to cultural studies, such as Sue Thornham's *Women, Feminism and Media* (2007). Applications such as these have been significant, useful, and innovative because they have provided methods for the interrogation of ideologies and their effect on a variety of representational modes, including literature and film. The notion of the "male gaze" has also been used in cultural studies, for example in *The Invisible Flâneuse? Gender, Public Space and Visual Culture in Nineteenth Century Paris* (2006) and in explorations of modern urban space in *Art, Space and the City: Public Art and Urban Features* (1997).[3]

Although the ideas in *Vision and Difference* have traveled far beyond the borders of art history, the intricacies of the text itself have been given the most attention by artists and art historians. Readers from other subjects are perhaps less inclined to deal with detailed readings of individual artworks, but these will always have relevance within artistic theory and practice. The themes expressed in *Vision and Difference* are also relevant to the evolving debates within gender studies and women's studies, and the book still has a considerable impact on contemporary feminist discourse. It has shaped the way that feminism is approached in an academic context, and demonstrates how issues in culture can be strongly connected to political activity.

Limitations

Vision and Difference does have some limitations in terms of its application, since it is rooted in primarily Western and middle-class experiences of vision and space. Pollock's assertion that patriarchal ideologies and visual imagery are connected is applicable the world over, yet her argument is mainly rooted in the European art tradition. Her consideration of gender is mainly limited to urban, cosmopolitan spaces and to some degree she expects her reader to have knowledge of these spaces. However, the text does refer to several universal themes, such as femininity, society, representation, teaching, and evaluation. These themes may not be explored on a global scale, but they are applicable to every modern civilization and can be adapted to suit individual circumstances. While Pollock uses examples from

European art history, it is entirely possible to apply many of her methods to artworks produced by any community in the world. Her criticisms of art history are also highly significant, and they demonstrate how the work of many art historians can be misogynistic* and biased toward male artists. Even if *Vision and Difference* did not rewrite the history of art for every culture, it at least encouraged these revisions to be written and suggested ways that this might be done.

NOTES

1   Rozsika Parker and Griselda Pollock, *Old Mistresses: Women, Art and Ideology* (London: Routledge & Kegan Paul, 1981), 3.

2   Griselda Pollock, *Vision and Difference: Feminism, Femininity and the Histories of Art* (London; New York: Routledge, 2003), xxvii.

3   Malcolm Miles, *Art, Space and the City: Public Art and Urban Features* (London: Routledge, 1997), 53.

MODULE 8
PLACE IN THE AUTHOR'S WORK

KEY POINTS

- *Vision and Difference* is one of several books that Griselda Pollock has written on gender and art.
- The text is a vital part of Pollock's corpus and it includes many of her most famous interpretations and ideas.
- It is certainly one of Pollock's best-known works.

Positioning

Griselda Pollock has described *Vision and Difference* as her "fifth feminist book thinking about and analyzing culture for inscriptions 'in, of and from the feminine'."[1] Among her previous works are the titles *Old Mistresses: Women, Art and Ideology*, *Framing Feminism: Art and the Women's Movement 1970–1985*, and *Dealing with Degas: Representations of Women and the Politics of Vision*. While these works pre-empted the content of *Vision and Difference*, many had been early, collaborative projects. *Vision and Difference* is a far more accomplished text, which demonstrates in detail Pollock's individual ideas and interests. It is Pollock's most widely read work, and gives a good representation of the ideas and interests that have dominated her career thus far. While Pollock has written several other texts, the popularity of *Vision and Difference* has meant that it is often the first book in her corpus that students will encounter. In this sense, it is her most important work.

Pollock and Rozsika Parker wrote *Old Mistresses* together; a work described by Pollock as their "opening feminist gambit."[2] The title refers to the female linguistic equivalent of "old master." The latter denotes a male artist who is highly respected, whereas the former

> ❝ I have spent thirty years or more thinking about feminist questions and art. Over twenty books and hundreds of articles bear witness to the sustained and long-term project involved in a feminist intervention. ❞
>
> Griselda Pollock, *Vision and Difference*, Routledge Classics edition

suggests a prostitute whose value is reduced due to her advanced years. As a product of patriarchy, language leaves little room for the female artist to be described or acknowledged. The text has a great deal in common with *Vision and Difference*, and expresses the same need to use feminism in order to revise the methods of the art historian. The aim of *Old Mistresses* is stated as: "[to] discover the history of women and art is in part to account for the way that art history is written. To expose its underlying values, its assumptions, its silences and its prejudices is also to understand that the way women artists are recorded is crucial to the definition of art and artist in our society."[3] Embryonic aspects of *Vision and Difference* can also be seen in Pollock's 1977 article "What's Wrong with Images of Women?" This text exposed the political and social narrative that exists underneath many visual representations of women.

Integration

Pollock's work is chiefly limited to the subject of feminist art history. While her approach and opinions develop over time, they remain consistent with one another. Seen as a whole, her corpus shows a gradual progression deeper into feminist art history.

Her PhD thesis focused on the male artist Vincent van Gogh and her first books were on Van Gogh and Jean François Millet. She then wrote a book on the female artist Mary Cassatt, which was followed by her first text on feminist art history, *Old Mistresses*. This latter work marked a turning point in her career, and defined her as a feminist art historian. After writing *Old Mistresses* and *Vision and Difference*, Pollock has written predominantly about women artists, and has tended to focus on lesser known figures who have previously been overlooked by art historians.

Vision and Difference is best read alongside *Old Mistresses* and *Differencing the Canon*, since all three provide slightly different perspectives on the same core ideas. Together, these three works create what the *Dictionary of Art Historians* calls Pollock's "triumvirate of feminist art theory."[4] Pollock herself describes *Old Mistresses* as her "opening feminist gambit" while she states that *Differencing the Canon* is "the book of my maturity."[5] That *Vision and Difference* was published in-between these two texts, suggests that developmentally, it is positioned between the two.

Significance

Vision and Difference is certainly one of Pollock's better-known works, and this is partly due to the fact that it is the one that is most easily applied to subjects outside of art history. It is often recommended reading for literature, media, and anthropology courses because the ideas it expounds can also be applied to language and other symbolic practices. Any form of representation will reproduce or comment upon the conditions in which it was produced, consequently they can provide a window into aspects of society—not least of all the treatment and experiences of women. *Vision and Difference* served as an example of how one might decode representations of the world.

While several of her other works argue for an art history that is free from the ideologies of patriarchy, *Vision and Difference* reinforced this view and articulated it with even more clarity. The book was the sum of all Pollock's previous efforts to describe and demonstrate feminist art history, and as such it serves as a clear indication of her ideas on the subject. It also marks an important moment in her career. While *Old Mistresses* helped to build her reputation, it was the success of *Vision and Difference* that sealed it. The fact that *Old Mistresses* was co-authored meant that Pollock's critical voice had been somewhat merged with Parker's, but *Vision and Difference* helped to showcase her own, individual, critical voice.

NOTES

1   Griselda Pollock, *Vision and Difference: Feminism, Femininity and the Histories of Art* (London; New York: Routledge, 2003), xvii.

2   Griselda Pollock, *Vision and Difference*, xxx.

3   Rozsika Parker and Griselda Pollock, *Old Mistresses: Women, Art and Ideology* (London: Routledge & Kegan Paul, 1981), 3.

4   Dictionary of Art Historians, https://dictionaryofarthistorians.org/pollockg.htm, accessed October 29, 2017.

5   Pollock, *Vision and Difference*, xxx.

SECTION 3
IMPACT

MODULE 9
THE FIRST RESPONSES

KEY POINTS

- *Vision and Difference* was successful on publication, but received some criticism for both its style and content.

- While Griselda Pollock did not respond directly to much of this criticism, her work did develop to in a way that suggests she accepted some of it.

- Griselda Pollock's work is now accepted as a product of its time.

Criticism

Griselda Pollock's *Vision and Difference* was generally welcomed by other researchers in the field of art history. One reviewer praised it as "one of the most substantial exercises in feminist revision of art historical practice,"[1] while another reviewer considered it "a vital text for understanding the polemics of feminist art history, and its methods and practice."[2]

While Pollock's approach was not revolutionary it still stood as an epitome of feminist criticism. While the details of Pollock's argument may have been unique to her, her overall argument captured the spirit of feminist art history at the time. A reviewer of the work highlighted this when he stated that the book "represents the vanguard of recent efforts to move beyond attempts to recover the histories of women artists [and] to examine instead the social structures (both of the past and of current historical practice) which cast 'women artists' as the exception to the rule."[3]

Despite its popularity, *Vision and Difference* has been subject to criticism, some of which is leveled at the style of the work. Clarity is paramount in a text with so many theories and ideas, but Pollock's style can make for what Carol Zemel* has called "a bumpy ride." She goes on to state that "*Vision and Difference* negotiates the confluence of theory, specific analyses, and feminist practice with some awkwardness of language … While some readers will find the tone bossy and the syntax prolix,* others no doubt will find her writing an audacious and thrilling call to arms."[4] Another problem raised by critics was Pollock's failure to address the question of pleasure. Many paintings are sexist but they are also beautiful, and some critics felt that there was a need for feminists to reconcile the issue of pleasure versus politics.[5] A further criticism of the text was that Pollock "read" the content and images rendered in paintings, but ignored factors such as style and medium. Frances S. Connelly* wrote "the argument on the whole suffers from a lack of attention to visual language. Style can and does carry meaning and ideology in a deeper and more fundamental way than content, but visual expression is consistently subordinated to verbal expression here."[6] Connelly was undoubtedly influenced in her criticisms by the fact that her own method uses exactly this kind of "visual language." She also expresses concerns about the limitations of the Marxist and Freudian models used by Pollock, and queries whether these would work outside of a Western context.

The issue of aesthetic pleasure is a significant criticism, but one which is exceptionally hard to resolve. If a picture is considered to be degrading to women, but is also deemed to be beautiful and pleasurable to look at, should it still be condemned? Zemel writes that "an ambivalence about pleasure haunts *Vision and Difference*" but notes that this is the case with "many feminist texts."[7] Many feminists will be conflicted in liking an image they know to be sexist, but which they find appealing for other reasons, such as its style or composition. The criticism of Pollock's style is a fair one, but the difficulty is not unexpected considering the complexity of her subject matter and the number of ideas she continuously keeps in play. Connolly's argument is perhaps the most convincing. While Pollock's command of "visual language" is superb, it is somewhat incomplete, and rarely looks beyond the factors of composition and subject matter. These aspects of the debate have now been addressed by critics such as Fiona Carson* and Claire Pajaczkowska* in their co-edited book *Feminist Visual Culture.*[8]

Responses

For unknown reasons, Pollock did not directly respond to the majority of negative criticisms of *Vision and Difference*. In her introduction to the new edition of the text, published in 2003, she mentions only one criticism in particular, which is that her work has been deemed out of date. She writes: "I have been told on more than one occasion that my work is 'history' now. That is, the debates have moved on to other questions such as internationalism, post-coloniality,* and post-gender studies of sexuality and queerness."* She does not reveal who has dealt these criticisms, but is quick to rebuff them, claiming that without the feminist interventions in art history many other debates would not be possible. Works such as *Vision and Difference* demonstrated how "knowledge is shaped in relations of power and invested with interests, political, ideological and psychological."[9] She argued that this forms the basic premise of many other approaches to art history and the humanities, and relates it to more than just a feminist argument.

It is possible that Pollock's later work was affected by the criticisms of *Vision and Difference*, but it is impossible to ascertain to what degree this is the case. Her next book-length publication was *Dealing with*

Degas: Representations of Women and the Politics of Vision (co-edited with Richard Kendall).[10] In a review of this book, Norma Broude noted that Pollock's contribution was "circuitously written and argued, [using] her now familiar strategies of segmentation and disjuncture."[11] From this it would appear that Pollock's style had not changed. Her approach is also similar, using psychoanalysis in particular to deconstruct Degas's imagery. One area in which Pollock may have responded to criticism is in the selection of images she chose to consider. In *Vision and Difference*, she chose to look at the representation of mainly white, middle-class women, consequently avoiding the complexity brought by incorporating issues of class and race, but this is something that changes in her later work. In *Differencing the Canon*, for example, she devotes a chapter to questioning whether white feminist discourse can be applied to black, post-colonial femininities without also oppressing them.[12] *Differencing the Canon* is also an example of how Pollock responded to positive criticism from those who wanted to know more about the nature of feminist art history and how it might influence other aspects of art history.

Conflict And Consensus

Despite the accusations that *Vision and Difference* is a difficult text, it was—and still is—widely read. Chapters of the books have been reprinted in anthologies of feminist criticism, and her chapter on "Modernity and the Spaces of Femininity" has been particularly influential. Using these anthologies, students have been able to read elements of the book, and approach its ideas through the more readable chapters. They are then in a better position to tackle the text as a whole. It is also helpful that Pollock's ideas have had time to enter into academic discourse, meaning that they are now less appear less confusing than they may have done to the original audience.

Many feminist art historians would identify with the ideas expressed in *Vision and Difference*. While some might not agree with

Pollock's theories or methods, the majority would have assented to Pollock's overarching sentiment, that feminism was a significant part of cultural history. The popularity and longevity of her work is partly due to the other academics working in her field. Griselda Pollock's ideas were sustained and accepted in part because of the combined work of other feminist art historians, such as Rozsika Parker, Fred Orton,* Laura Mulvey, and Lucy Lippard.*

NOTES

1 Mira Schor, *Wet: On Painting, Feminism and Art Culture* (Durham, NC: Duke University Press, 1997), 106.

2 Anthea Callen, University of Nottingham, in Griselda Pollock, *Vision and Difference: Feminism, Femininity and the Histories of Art* (London; New York: Routledge, 2003), front endpapers.

3 Frances S. Connelly, *The Journal of Aesthetics and Art Criticism*, 49.1 (Winter, 1991), 81–83.

4 Carol Zemel, "Review of *Vision and Difference*," *The Art Bulletin* 72.2 (June 1990), 336–41.

5 Zemel, "Review of *Vision and Difference*," 336–41.

6 Frances S. Connelly, "Review of *Vision and Difference*," *The Journal of Aesthetics and Art Criticism,* Vol 49, No. 1, (Winter 1991), 81–3.

7 Zemel, "Review of *Vision and Difference*," 340.

8 Fiona Carson and Claire Pajaczkowska, eds., *Feminist Visual Culture* (Edinburgh: Edinburgh University Press, 2000).

9 Griselda Pollock, *Vision and Difference: Feminism, Femininity and the Histories of Art* (London; New York: Routledge, 2003), xix.

10 Richard Kendall and Griselda Pollock, eds., *Dealing with Degas: Representations of Women and the Politics of Vision* (London: Pandora Books, 1992).

11 Norma Broude, "Review of *Dealing with Degas*," *Women's Art Journal,* 16.2 (Autumn 1995–Winter 1996), 38.

12 Griselda Pollock, *Differencing the Canon: Feminist Desire and the Writing of Art's Histories*. (London: Routledge, 1999).

MODULE 10
THE EVOLVING DEBATE

KEY POINTS

- *Vision and Difference* forms a key element of Griselda Pollock's corpus.
- The text has had an effect on schools of thought both in and outside of academia.
- It is a part of current scholarship across the humanities.

Uses And Problems

The ideas Griselda Pollock proposed in Vision and Difference help form a central part of her work, and the book can be seen as the foundation stone for much of her later writing. In particular, *Vision and Difference* stands witness to its author's belief in the importance of feminist art history to the women's movement, and demonstrates at length the methods of analysis that have become so much a part of her work. *Vision and Difference* is not the only work by Pollock to deal with the subject of feminist art history, but it was her first book to be successful outside of the subject of art history. This success may have influenced the writing of her later work, since *Vision and Difference* had proven that there was an audience for Pollock's ideas.

Vision and Difference helped to define and develop the subject of feminist art history, and much of the research in this area has benefited from Pollock's direct involvement. For example, the text *Generations and Geographies in the Visual Arts*,[1] a collection edited by Pollock, builds on many of the ideas she raises in *Vision and Difference*. These include an interdisciplinary approach and a consideration of visual and physical space. *Vision and Difference* has also been used to analyze gender in urban spaces,[2] and to negotiate images and concepts of the erotic in

> **❝** Feminism "is a way of thinking." **❞**
>
> Griselda Pollock, *Vision and Difference*, Routledge Classics edition

art.[3] Pollock further examined the politics of viewing art in her book *Encounters in the Virtual Feminist Museum*.

Schools Of Thought

Pollock's ideas have had an indirect effect on mainstream feminism, particularly on the notion that women have the right to be represented realistically and on their own terms. Examples of this are the recent Dove© advertising campaign, which challenged the way that women were being represented in the media.[4] Another example is the 2006 collection of poetry entitled *Images of Women*, which Myra Schneider* and Dilys Wood* edited. The preface to the poetry collection claims that "[these] images of women are images of women by women, constructed out of twenty-first century consciousness, unmediated by the male gaze."[5] The desire to avoid the gaze of men and to be in control of female imagery is an important aspect of Pollock's work, and *Vision and Difference* contributed to placing these into the mainstream.

Not surprisingly, Pollock's *Vision and Difference* has contributed to gender studies and feminist art history, and it undoubtedly shaped the subject of art history as we know it today. Her call for a "feminist intervention in the histories of art" did not go unnoticed, and feminist art criticism continues to develop while more women artists are being studied than ever before.[6] However, Pollock feels that people "still misrecognize feminism as a merely historical phenomenon, limited to a certain time and place," and she argued that feminist theory still needs to be more widely understood as a "radical questioning, a way of thinking."[7]

In Current Scholarship

The themes and ideas expressed in *Vision and Difference* firmly place the text within the category of feminist art history. However, its far-reaching implications mean it can also exist comfortably in the categories of psychology, history, social studies, and cultural studies. The themes expressed in *Vision and Difference* are also highly relevant to gender studies and women's studies. By considering the visual representation of women, and their treatment by art historians, Pollock exposes a significant aspect of feminism that does not simply apply to students of art history. Her analysis of the way art history is written relates to the writing of history more generally, and questions why women are written out of historical accounts of the past. In addition, her evaluation of the artistic depiction of women proves how important images can be in the construction of gender roles, and in the deconstruction* of these roles by feminist artists.

Current proponents of the kinds of analysis carried out in *Vision and Difference* believe in the book's assertion that political and cultural factors are innately connected, and that all processes and methods of critical and artistic production need to be questioned rather than blindly accepted. This support of the text often extends to an endorsement of Pollock's materialist* attitude to research, which takes social and economic factors into account when assessing the nature of an artwork. The book's focus on discourses of power, and on the visual representation of repressed and marginalized communities, is useful for researchers interested in queer theory, post-colonialism, and studies of class. While these uses of the text may divert from its feminist origins, they are still in accordance with Pollock's basic argument for an interrogation of ideologies.

Several writers and thinkers have been inspired by *Vision and Difference*, some in direct and others in indirect ways. Books such as *The Invisible Flâneuse? Gender, Public Space and Visual Culture in Nineteenth Century Paris*, and *Art, Space and the City: Public Art and*

Urban Features, use the text directly in order to help build their theories about gender and the environment. These thinkers particularly draw on the chapter in *Vision and Difference* entitled "Modernity and the Spaces of Femininity," and on its evaluation of gender and space. Researchers working on periods and cultures outside modern America and Europe have also been able to use *Vision and Difference* in their work. For example, Israel Gershoni,* Hakan Erdem,* and Ursula Woköck* make reference to it in their edited collection *Histories of the Modern Middle East,*[8] and Joan DelPlato* uses it in her analysis of orientalist* representations of the harem.[9]

NOTES

1   Griselda Pollock, ed., *Generations and Geographies in the Visual Arts: Feminist Readings.* (London: Routledge, 1996).

2   Aruna D'Souza and Tom McDonough, eds., *The Invisible Flâneuse? Gender, Public Space and Visual Culture in Nineteenth Century Paris* (Manchester: Manchester University Press, 2006).

3   Helen McDonald, *Erotic Ambiguities; The Female Nude in Art* (London: Routledge, 2001), 81–5.

4   Steven M. Kates and Glenda Shaw-Garlock, "The Ever Entangling Web: A Study of Ideologies and Discourses in Advertising to Women," *Journal of Advertising* 28.2 (Summer 1999), 33–49.

5   Myra Schneider and Dilys Wood, eds., *Images of Women* (California: Arrowhead Press, 2006).

6   Pollock, Griselda. *Differencing the Canon: Feminist Desire and the Writing of Art's* Histories. London: Routledge, 1999. 24.

7   Pollock, *Vision and Difference,* xx.

8   Israel Gershoni, Hakan Erdem and Ursula Woköck, eds., *Histories of the Modern Middle East* (Boulder, Colorado: Rienner, 2002), 89.

9   Joan DelPlato, *Multiple Wives, Multiple Pleasures: Representing the Harem 1800–1875* (London: Rosemont, 2002), 247.

MODULE 11
IMPACT AND INFLUENCE TODAY

KEY POINTS

- *Vision and Difference* by Griselda Pollock has been a successful text across the humanities.
- The work still forms a part of contemporary debate.
- The debate over the place of feminism in the humanities still continues.

Position

Several ideas proposed in Griselda Pollock's *Vision and Difference* have proved highly significant in a wider setting, and have contributed to the shaping of popular feminist political and academic writing. By considering the visual representation of women, and their treatment by art historians, Pollock exposed a significant aspect of political feminism that does not simply apply to students of art history. Her analysis of the way art history is written relates to the writing of history more generally, and questions why women are written out of historical accounts. In addition, her evaluation of the artistic depiction of women proves how important images can be in the construction of gender roles, and in the deconstruction of these roles by feminist artists. All of this has had an impact on the way that women artists are treated and the way that art historians evaluate their work. While *Vision and Difference* alone did not effect these changes in attitude, the book does provide a point of access to other works in a similar vein, and has helped to promote a particular aspect of feminist work.

Since its publication in 1988, *Vision and Difference* has proven consistently successful. It has gained in popularity within literary studies, but further work done by Pollock and others has meant that the text is

> **❝** *Vision and Difference* remains amongst the most important and thought-provoking feminist interventions in art history. **❞**
>
> Anthea Callen, University of Nottingham, 2005, reprinted in *Vision and Difference*, Routledge Classics edition.

slightly less influential in gender studies. Its reissue as a "classic" by Routledge Classics in 2003 is both a positive and negative development. On the one hand, it cements the text's success and popularity, but as Pollock writes in her introduction to the edition, the label of "classic" has damaging implications. She argued that "[it] is as if there is a will to cast feminist work in, and on, the histories of art back into the momentarily ruffled surface of the history of the late 20th century as an intellectual curiosity, no longer relevant to current practices."[1]

Interaction

Vision and Difference still plays a part in debates about the place of feminism in the humanities. Pollock's work is designed to demonstrate that feminism is not an optional extra for courses that would otherwise be male-dominated and that simply studying female artists does not immediately make a course feminist. In *Vision and Difference* Pollock argues that gender should not be omitted from mainstream art history, and calls for a shift in thinking and objectives among her academic colleagues. Quoting Linda Nochlin, Pollock argues "the so-called woman question, far from being a peripheral sub-issue, can become a catalyst … providing links with paradigms established by radical approaches in other fields."[2] This debate is relatively widespread, and relates to the use of feminism in other areas, particularly the study of history, film, literature studies, and psychology. It can be used to re-evaluate not only the content of academic courses but the methods and techniques that are taught.

The attention that *Vision and Difference* receives is mainly based on its status as a major work of feminist criticism. Many researchers respond to the text by building on its already established ideas, and refining them to suit different circumstances and subjects. Pollock herself is sometimes involved in this process, and edits, co-edits and contributes to collections of research that build on the core ideas outlined in *Vision and Difference*.[3] The expanding project of feminist art history is motivated by both political and professional ambitions. Feminism is a political movement, and many feminist academics are motivated by their desire for gender equality as well as by their desire to produce research. However, taken in their entirety, Pollock's ideas pose difficulties for those wishing to apply them to an institutional context when designing a course. She examines ideology so rigorously that social or political concerns could overwhelm any focus on artworks, resulting in a course more like cultural or political studies than art history.

The Continuing Debate

Although *Vision and Difference* has been subsumed into the foundations of art history as a subject, many of its recommendations (such as making feminism a more prominent part of art history, and revising the methods of the art historian) have not been adopted across the board. The challenge that the text serves to existing teaching methods within art history remains as vigorous as it always was, and while feminism is often taught on art history courses it is still sometimes viewed as an add-on or optional extra. *Vision and Difference* still encourages students to study the ideology behind the way art history is formulated and taught. It also prompts a revaluation of the way similar subjects in the humanities are taught, in particular history and literature, which have been restricted by a male bias in the past.

As a text that was published only a few decades ago, *Vision and Difference* has retained a great deal of its relevance. The application of feminism to subjects in the humanities is still a significant issue, and feminist readings of history more generally are still being developed. The usefulness of the text has been enhanced by the debate that surrounded and fostered Pollock's writing; this includes the work of Rozsika Parker, Fred Orton, Laura Mulvey, and Lucy Lippard. These thinkers have built around and on the work done by Pollock (sometimes in collaboration with Pollock herself) and have given the text a stronger academic setting, consequently making the text a more useful and significant tool for researchers.

The positive and negative attributes of *Vision and Difference* have shifted in response to changing attitudes and ideas. Pollock's feminism was once read as a "thrilling call to arms,"[4] but it has lost some of its impact now that art history courses further incorporate studies of gender and ideology. It may be that modern readers see the situation as resolved, or they see the emphasis on feminism as dated and want to use similar methods to analyze race or class instead. Pollock's methods as an art historian may be considered in a more positive light now that so many approaches to art history (such as post-colonial or queer readings) rely on the type of Marxist, or psychological reading Pollock demonstrates in *Vision and Difference*.

NOTES

1   Griselda Pollock, *Vision and Difference: Feminism, Femininity and the Histories of Art* (London; New York: Routledge, 2003), xviii.

2   Pollock, *Vision and Difference*, 2.

3   Examples are *Framing Feminism: Art and the Women's Movement* 1970–1985 (London: Pandora, 1987) and *Generations and Geographies in the Visual Arts: Feminist Readings* (London: Routledge, 1996).

4   Carol Zemel, "Review of *Vision and Difference*," *The Art Bulletin* 72.2 (June 1990): 336–41.

MODULE 12
WHERE NEXT?

KEY POINTS

* *Vision and Difference* by Griselda Pollock is starting to be seen as a "classic" text.

* While feminism is still a vital part of the debate, the study of power relations has expanded to include post-colonialism, queer theory, and class dynamics.

* The text is a classic work of feminist theory, and of significant importance in the study of art history.

Potential

Griselda Pollock's *Vision and Difference* is a highly influential book that has retired somewhat to the status of a seminal or classic work. This is especially the case in the fields of art history, film theory, and feminist theory, where the book is viewed as "a foundational text."[1] The decision of Routledge Classics to reissue it as a "classic" in 2003 had positive and negative effects. On the one hand, it highlighted the book's success, but on the other it also perhaps had the effect of consigning it to history, causing it to be challenged or interrogated less than it otherwise would be.

Vision and Difference can be said to have lost some of its relevance, since it reflects a particular moment in the history of equality, and typifies a stage in the development of feminist writing and debate. Yet this makes the text relevant in different ways, as it gains a reputation for being a historical document it will become increasingly useful to students wishing to study the history of feminist thought. Chapters such as "Screening the Seventies" can be used to understand the social and political impact of feminism in the 1970s and 1980s.

> **❝I have been told on more than one occasion that my work is 'history' now.❞**
> Griselda Pollock, *Vision and Difference*, Routledge Classics edition

The book is ready to be re-examined, and will benefit from being read in different contexts. Subject areas that do not currently study *Vision and Difference*—such as political science—may benefit from the contributions it has to make, in particular its commentary on the production of power. It will also have increasing relevance to contemporary culture as many modern societies become more and more reliant on images to communicate social values and ideas.

Taken out of a strictly feminist context, Pollock's ideas could speak to a broad range of research subjects. Pollock's methods can be applied to current and future forms of representation, such as images of women on the internet or in video games. It can also play a role in our analysis of advertising and propaganda, and provide a way of understanding how gender might be used to convince audiences of an idea or opinion. *Vision and Difference* can also be used to read representations of race and class, since it essentially provides a way of understanding the representation of repressed or marginalized groups.

Future Directions

Pollock herself acknowledges that the debate about power relations and the politics of representation, has evolved to include "other questions such as internationalism, postcoloniality, and post-gender studies of sexuality and queerness."[2] However, she points out these discussions have been made possible in part through feminist scholars, and their assertion "that knowledge is shaped in relations of power and invested with interests, political, ideological and psychological."[3] She accepts that feminism was never alone in making this claim, but argues that feminist interoperations laid the groundwork for investigating power relations in a broader context. It is true that the future of art history will involve more than simply feminist theory, but since Pollock's ideas are ultimately rooted in the study of representation and ideology, it easily translates to other projects that are not strictly concerned with gender inequality.

The feminist debate itself has developed since *Vision and Difference* was first published. As forms of representation change, and arguably become more influential than they have ever been, the work will have a new kind of relevance. In light of platforms such as Instagram and Facebook, the issue of self-representation becomes increasingly important. Women are choosing to present themselves in certain ways, and it is important to understand the visual language that they use and why they are drawn to it. As culture is becoming ever more reliant on the use of visual images in order to communicate, advertise, and entertain, Pollock's ideas have become increasingly important. Books exploring this issue have only recently been published, and the debate continues to grow in importance.[4]

Summary

Vision and Difference has fueled wider debate, particularly in relation to art history, feminist theory, and film theory. Pollock's argument that the process of representation is a political act, is easily applied to other representative art-forms. Her work highlighted the degree to which patriarchal ideologies were dependent on visual images, and gave viewers the tools with which to decode and analyze these images. While books such as *Vision and Difference* have helped guide the debate over how women are represented, it is clear that women are still being depicted in derogatory ways by the fashion and media industries. Painters and sculptors are now less likely to portray the female form in the way the Pre-Raphaelites did, yet fashion models are still presented in a way that echoes paintings from this period. The majority of visual images that are produced and disseminated are of women, and a large proportion of these are of celebrities and fashion models. Instead of a paintbrush, the artist now uses make-up, lighting, and digital enhancement in order to achieve a certain level of perfection that is far removed from the reality,

Ultimately, *Vision and Difference* had the greatest impact on the discipline of art history. It not only questioned the misogyny inherent in the production of many artworks, but also challenged the overwhelmingly male perspective that was being reproduced in art criticism and research. Pollock's work, and that of other feminist scholars, helped to challenge the way that art history was being taught, and gave students new methods to work with. Yet the book can still be a catalyst for further change. In her introduction to the new edition of the text, Pollock hopes that the book will "find new readers, open to and desiring ... a difference to thought, to art, to culture, and to society," and that they will make this change "joyously, and at times, angrily with all sorts of women in mind."[5]

NOTES

1   Grant Pooke and Diana Newall, *Art History: The Basics* (London: Routledge, 2008), 162.

2   Griselda Pollock, *Vision and Difference: Feminism, Femininity and the Histories of Art* (London; New York: Routledge, 2003), xix.

3   Pollock, *Vision and Difference*, xix.

4   Karen Ross and Carolyn M. Byerly, *Women and Media: International Interpretations* (London: Blackwell, 2008).

5   Pollock, *Vision and Difference*, xxxviii.

GLOSSARY

GLOSSARY OF TERMS

Cultural studies: an academic discipline which emerged in Britain in the 1960s, comprised of several different approaches and methods, typically focused on contemporary culture and on its historical, social, and political foundations.

Deconstruction: a movement in philosophy that questions traditional assumptions about truth and certainty. When applied to literature or film studies, it typically attempts to expose the inherent contradictions in a film or a text by delving below its surface meaning. In a more general sense it can refer to the dismantling and examination of ideas or works.

Femininity: a term used to describe the roles, attributes, and behaviors that are traditionally associated with girls and women. It is not gender-specific, and can be displayed by both men and women. It is a social and cultural construct, and can be shaped and reinforced through language, the media, and the visual arts.

Feminism: a political concept that can be used to denote a number of movements and ideologies. While there are variations within feminism, it broadly concerns the establishment and defense of equal political, social, and economic rights for both sexes. It particularly concerns the rights of women.

First-wave feminism: a feminist movement that existed in the late nineteenth and early twentieth centuries. First-wave feminists were chiefly concerned with fighting for women's legal rights, including their right to vote in elections.

Freudian: refers to the ideas of Sigmund Freud (1856–1939), an Austrian neurologist and the founding father of psychoanalysis.

Gender studies: concerns the analysis of gendered identity and representations of gender. It is an interdisciplinary subject and may involve aspects of sociology, psychology, political science, media studies, and history. Sociology is the study of the development, structure, and functioning of human society.

Ideology: refers to a set of ideas proposed by the ruling sections of society to the rest of society.

Impressionism: a nineteenth-century artistic movement that used tones and broad brush strokes to give an overall impression rather than fine detail. It originated in Paris.

London Women's Art History Collective: an organization of women who wanted art history to be a part of a wider social and political feminist movement. It emerged out of a public meeting that had been organized in support of the Swedish artist Monica Sjoo (1938–2005), who was being prosecuted for obscenity after having exhibited her painting *God Giving Birth* in 1971. Griselda Pollock and Rozsika Parker were founding members of the collective.

Marxism: a social, political and economic worldview that can be used as a method for understanding cultures and histories. It is based on a materialist interpretation of social and economic development.

Materialism: (or a materialist perspective) puts emphasis on the physical objects and processes that contribute to situation or idea. Historical materialism, for example, is a study of history made through the physical objects that comprised that history (buildings, artifacts, landscapes, and so on).

Media studies: an academic subject that deals with the content and history of media in their various forms. Media studies is particularly concerned with mechanized forms of communication that have a mass audience, such as film, television, and radio. It is less focused on traditional forms, such as theater, painting, and literature.

Misogyny: prejudice towards women or a hatred or dislike of women.

Orientalist: someone engaged the study of oriental cultures and histories.

Paradigm: a pattern or model; a concept within which something is explored. A typical example.

Patriarchy: a society or culture where a set of ideas is proposed and enforced for the benefit of sustaining male dominance.

Post-colonialism: literally means "after colonialism." The analysis of colonialism and imperialism in the past and present.

Pre-Raphaelite movement: a British nineteenth-century movement led by the Pre-Raphaelite Brotherhood—a group of artists, poets, and designers. Its members aimed to reject modern forms of production and return to the aesthetics that existed before the work of the Italian painter Raphael (1483–1520)—hence the name, Pre-Raphaelite.

Production of knowledge: refers to the argument that all knowledge is subject to the medium through which it is produced, and to the society that produces it; while some facts may be hard to dispute, the process of communicating them can cause these facts to become political.

Prolix: of long or overlong duration.

Psychology/psychoanalysis: a way of understanding human behavior in relation to the unconscious mind where automatic processes relate to factors such as thought, memory, and dreams, and are mostly unrecognized by the conscious mind. These automatic processes can be universal, or they can be affected by personal circumstances.

Queer: in academia the terms queerness, queer or queering are used to refer to the study of social and cultural areas from a non-heteronormative perspective (one in which matters are not automatically seen through the eyes of a heterosexual). It often involves considering these areas in the light of homosexuality and bisexuality.

Second-wave feminism: this women's liberation movement extended roughly from the 1960s to the 1980s. As with the first wave, it was primarily concerned with obtaining equal rights for women. A distinctive element of the second-wave movement was that cultural and political inequalities were seen as being inextricably linked, and work such as Pollock's contributed to this aspect considerably.

Semiotics the study of science and symbols, and of communication through the interpretation of signs and symbols, particularly language.

Sexism: a prejudice against someone based on their gender.

Sociology: the study of the organization, structure, development, and functioning of human society.

Third-wave feminist movement: a movement considered to have begun during the 1990s and continues through to the present day. While it grew out of the second-wave feminist movement, it began to incorporate more women who may not have identified with feminism previously.

The women's movement: a broad term that typically refers to the development of feminist politics in the twentieth and twenty-first centuries.

PEOPLE MENTIONED IN THE TEXT

John Berger (1926–2017) is an English critic, artist, and novelist. He wrote *Ways of Seeing* (London: BBC Enterprises, 1972). It was based on a BBC television series he made with English documentary filmmaker Mike Dibb (born 1940), and demonstrated that throughout history women have been depicted in art as being looked at, and men have been depicted as the ones with visual agency—those who gaze at and examine the bodies of women.

Norma Broude (b. 1941) is an American feminist art historian who specializes in nineteenth-century French and Italian painting.

Fiona Carson is a British feminist art historian and artist.

Mary Cassatt (1844–1926) was an American painter and printmaker who lived most of her life in France. She employed the style of the Impressionist movement, and often depicted the private and social lives of women and children.

Deborah Cherry (b. 1949) is a feminist art historian, who is currently Professor of the History of Art at the University of Sussex.

Frances S. Connelly (b. 1953) is an American feminist art historian.

Timothy James (T. J.) Clark (b. 1943) is an English Marxist art historian and writer. His article "On the Conditions of Artistic Creation" (*Times Literary Supplement*, May 24, 1974, 561–3) argued that art history needed to deconstruct the ideology of the privileged masculine individual.

Elizabeth Cowie is a feminist anthropologist. Her article "Woman as Sign" (*m/f* 1.1, 1978, 50) particularly influenced Pollock. It emphasized the importance of signifying systems in the production of gender difference, and suggested that images of women were often signs and symbols for social meanings, instead of being merely representations of a human being.

Edgar Degas (1834–1917) was a French Impressionist artist, who was particularly famous for his paintings of ballet dancers.

Joan DelPlato (b. 1953) is a professor of art history and women's studies.

Hakan Erdem (b. 1962) is a historian who has written about the Ottoman Empire.

Michel Foucault (1926–1984) was a French literary critic, philosopher, and historian of ideas. His main concern was the relationship between power and knowledge, particularly the ways in which those in power control and produce knowledge.

Sigmund Freud (1856–1939) was an Austrian neurologist and the founding father of psychoanalysis.

Mary Garrard (b. 1937) is an American feminist art historian, who has written extensively on feminism and art. She is an emerita professor at the American University.

Israel Gershoni (b. 1946) is a historian of Middle Eastern and African history at the University of Tel Aviv.

Germaine Greer (b. 1939) is a controversial Australian feminist, most famous for her feminist work, *The Female Eunuch*.

Eva Hesse (1936–70) was a Jewish, German-born, American sculptor. She was known for working with a number of new and exciting materials.

Mary Kelly (b. 1941) is an American conceptualist artist, feminist, and academic.

Lucy Lippard (b. 1937) is a highly influential American art critic, writer, curator, and feminist.

Edouard Manet (1832–83) was a French painter who played a significant role in the development of the Impressionist movement.

Jean François Millet (1814–1875) was a French painter who was well-known for his images of farmers and peasants.

Kate Millett (1934–2017) was a feminist activist and writer, best known for her book *Sexual Politics* (1970) which was a large influence on feminism at the time.

Karl Marx (1818–83) was a German social scientist and founding father of socialism.

Berthe Morisot (1841–95) was a female French painter belonging to the Impressionist movement.

Laura Mulvey (b. 1941) is a British feminist and film theorist.

Linda Nochlin (b. 1931) is an American art historian, considered to be a leader in the field of feminist art history studies.

Fred Orton (b. 1949) is a British writer and researcher of art history.

Claire Pajaczkowska is an independent filmmaker and academic.

Rozsika Parker (1945–2010) was an English psychotherapist, art historian, writer and feminist.

Jacqueline Rose (b. 1949) is an English literary critic and academic who is currently Professor of English at Queen Mary University of London.

Dante Gabriel Rossetti (1828–82) was a British artist, poet, and translator. His paintings typified the work of the Pre-Raphaelite Brotherhood, of which he was a key member.

Charlotte Saloman (1917–43) was a German Jewish artist, who created a series of autobiographical paintings titled "Life? or Theatre? A Song-play."

Myra Schneider (b. 1936) is a British poet and author of fiction.

Elizabeth Siddall (1829–62) was an English poet, artist, and artist's model, who was painted extensively by members of the Pre-Raphaelite Brotherhood.

Monica Sjoo (1938–2005) was a Swedish artist and feminist, whose work centered on neo-pagan folklore and the celebration of female empowerment.

Vincent van Gogh (1853–80) was a French Post-Impressionist painter, whose lively landscapes and still lives used color and form in new and expressive ways.

Ursula Woköck is a cultural historian who writes about the colonial history of Germany.

Dilys Wood is a British poet.

Carol Zemel is an American feminist art historian. She is currently Professor of Visual Art and Art History at the University of York, Toronto.

WORKS CITED

WORKS CITED

Berger, John. *Ways of Seeing*. London: BBC Enterprises, 1972.

Broude, Norma. "Review of *Vision and Difference* by Griselda Pollock." *Women's Art Journal* 16.2 (Autumn 1995–Winter 1996): 35–40.

Broude, Norma, and Mary Garrard, eds. *Feminism and Art History: Questioning the Litany*. New York: Harper & Row, 1982.

Byerly, Carolyn M., and Karen Ross. *Women and Media: International Interpretations*. London: Blackwell, 2008.

Carson, Fiona, and Claire Pajaczkowska. *Feminist Visual Culture*. Edinburgh: Edinburgh University Press, 2000.

Clark, Timothy James. "On the Conditions of Artistic Creation." *Times Literary Supplement*, May 24, 1974, 561–3.

Code, Lorraine, ed. *Routledge Encyclopedia of Feminist Theories.* London: Routledge, 2000.

Connelly, Frances S., "Review of Griselda Pollock's *Vision and Difference*." *The Journal of Aesthetics and Art Criticism,* 49.1 (Winter, 1991), 81–83.

Cowie, Elizabeth. "Woman as Sign." *m/f* 1.1 (1978): 50.

DelPlato, Joan. *Multiple Wives, Multiple Pleasures, Representing the Harem 1800–1875*. London: Rosemont, 2002.

D'Souza, Aruna, and Tom McDonough, eds. *The Invisible Flâneuse? Gender, Public Space and Visual Culture in Nineteenth-Century Paris*. Manchester: Manchester University Press, 2006.

Foucault, Michel, *The History of Sexuality V I: The Will to Knowledge* (London: Penguin, 1998).

Friedan, Betty. *The Feminine Mystique*. London: W.W. Norton and Co., 1963.

Gershoni, Israel, Hakan Erdem, and Ursula Woköck, eds. *Histories of the Modern Middle East*. Boulder, Colorado: Rienner, 2002.

Greer, Germaine, *The Female Eunuch*. London: MacGibbon & Kee, 1970.

The Obstacle Race: The Fortunes of Women Painters and Their Work. London: Secker and Warburg, 1979.

Hawksley, Lucinda. *Lizzie Siddal: Face of the Pre-Raphaelites*. New York: Walker, 2006.

Humm, Maggie. *Border Traffic: Strategies of Contemporary Women Writers*.

Manchester: Manchester University Press, 1991.

Jagodzinski, Jan. *Pun(k) Deconstruction: Experifigural Writings in Art and Education*. London: Routledge, 1997.

Kates, Steven M., and Glenda Shaw-Garlock. "The Ever Entangling Web: A study of Ideologies and Discourses in Advertising to Women." *Journal of Advertising* Volume 28, No.2 (Summer 1999): 33–49.

Kelly, Mary, "Desiring Images/Imaging Desire." *Wedge*, no. 6 (1986): 5–9.

Langford, Rachael, ed., *Textual Intersections: Literature, History and the Arts in Nineteenth-Century Europe*. Amsterdam: Rodopi, 2009.

Marx, Karl, *A Contribution to the Critique of Political Economy*. Chicago: Charles H. Kerr & Co., 1904.

McDonald, Helen. *Erotic Ambiguities: The Female Nude in Art*. London: Routledge, 2001.

Miles, Malcolm. *Art, Space and the City: Public Art and Urban Features*. London: Routledge, 1997.

Murray, Chris, ed. *Key Writers on Art: The Twentieth Century*. London: Routledge, 2003.

Nelmes, Jill, ed. *Introduction to Film Studies*. London: Routledge, 2001.

Nochlin, Linda "Why Have There Been No Great Women Artists?" *ARTnews* (January 1971) reprinted in *The Feminism and Visual Culture Reader,* 2nd ed. (London: Routledge, 2003) 263–267.

Parker, Rozsika, and Griselda Pollock, eds. *Framing Feminism: Art and the Women's Movement 1970–1985*. London: Pandora, 1987.

Old Mistresses: Women, Art and Ideology. London: Routledge & Kegan Paul, 1981.

Pollock, Griselda. *Differencing the Canon: Feminist Desire and the Writing of Art's Histories*. London: Routledge, 1999.

--- "Inscriptions in the Feminine." In *Inside the Visible: An Elliptical Traverse of Twentieth-Century Art In, Of, and From the Feminine*, edited by Catherine de Zegher. Cambridge, Massachusetts: MIT Press, 1996.

--- "Is Feminism to Judaism as Modernity is to Tradition? Critical questions on Jewishness, Femininity and Art." In Rubies and Rebels: Jewish Female Identity in Contemporary British Art, edited by Monica Bohm-Duchen and Vera Grodzinski, 15–27. London: Lund Humphries, 1996.

--- *Vision and Difference: Feminism, Femininity and the Histories of Art*. London; New York: Routledge Classics, 2003.

--- "What's Wrong with Images of Women?" *Screen Education* (No. 24): 25–34.

Pollock, Griselda, ed. *Generations and Geographies in the Visual Arts: Feminist Readings.* London: Routledge, 1996.

Pollock, Griselda, and Richard Kendall, eds. *Dealing with Degas: Representations of Women and the Politics of Vision*. London: Pandora Books, 1992.

Pooke, Grant, and Diana Newall. *Art History: The Basics*. London: Routledge, 2007.

Rose, Jacqueline. *Sexuality in the Field of Vision*. London: Verso, 1986.

Schor, Mira. *Wet: On Painting, Feminism and Art Culture*. Durham, NC: Duke University Press, 1997.

Schneider, Myra, and Dilys Wood. *Images of Women by Contemporary Women Poets*. California: Arrowhead Press, 2006.

Thornham, Sue. *Women, Feminism and Media*. Edinburgh: Edinburgh University Press, 2007.

Tyler, Christian. "Sex Secrets of Art History." Interview with Griselda Pollock. *Financial Times*, February 6th, 1993. Issue 31982, WFT22 (1).

UNESCO Report. "Getting the Balance Right: Gender Equality in Journalism." Belgium: International Federation of Journalists, 2009.

Zemel, Carol. "Review of *Vision and Difference*." *The Art Bulletin* 72.2 (June 1990): 336–41.

THE MACAT LIBRARY
BY DISCIPLINE

AFRICANA STUDIES

Chinua Achebe's *An Image of Africa: Racism in Conrad's Heart of Darkness*
W. E. B. Du Bois's *The Souls of Black Folk*
Zora Neale Huston's *Characteristics of Negro Expression*
Martin Luther King Jr's *Why We Can't Wait*
Toni Morrison's *Playing in the Dark: Whiteness in the American Literary Imagination*

ANTHROPOLOGY

Arjun Appadurai's *Modernity at Large: Cultural Dimensions of Globalisation*
Philippe Ariès's *Centuries of Childhood*
Franz Boas's *Race, Language and Culture*
Kim Chan & Renée Mauborgne's *Blue Ocean Strategy*
Jared Diamond's *Guns, Germs & Steel: the Fate of Human Societies*
Jared Diamond's *Collapse: How Societies Choose to Fail or Survive*
E. E. Evans-Pritchard's *Witchcraft, Oracles and Magic Among the Azande*
James Ferguson's *The Anti-Politics Machine*
Clifford Geertz's *The Interpretation of Cultures*
David Graeber's *Debt: the First 5000 Years*
Karen Ho's *Liquidated: An Ethnography of Wall Street*
Geert Hofstede's *Culture's Consequences: Comparing Values, Behaviors, Institutes and Organizations across Nations*
Claude Lévi-Strauss's *Structural Anthropology*
Jay Macleod's *Ain't No Makin' It: Aspirations and Attainment in a Low-Income Neighborhood*
Saba Mahmood's *The Politics of Piety: The Islamic Revival and the Feminist Subject*
Marcel Mauss's *The Gift*

BUSINESS

Jean Lave & Etienne Wenger's *Situated Learning*
Theodore Levitt's *Marketing Myopia*
Burton G. Malkiel's *A Random Walk Down Wall Street*
Douglas McGregor's *The Human Side of Enterprise*
Michael Porter's *Competitive Strategy: Creating and Sustaining Superior Performance*
John Kotter's *Leading Change*
C. K. Prahalad & Gary Hamel's *The Core Competence of the Corporation*

CRIMINOLOGY

Michelle Alexander's *The New Jim Crow: Mass Incarceration in the Age of Colorblindness*
Michael R. Gottfredson & Travis Hirschi's *A General Theory of Crime*
Richard Herrnstein & Charles A. Murray's *The Bell Curve: Intelligence and Class Structure in American Life*
Elizabeth Loftus's *Eyewitness Testimony*
Jay Macleod's *Ain't No Makin' It: Aspirations and Attainment in a Low-Income Neighborhood*
Philip Zimbardo's *The Lucifer Effect*

ECONOMICS

Janet Abu-Lughod's *Before European Hegemony*
Ha-Joon Chang's *Kicking Away the Ladder*
David Brion Davis's *The Problem of Slavery in the Age of Revolution*
Milton Friedman's *The Role of Monetary Policy*
Milton Friedman's *Capitalism and Freedom*
David Graeber's *Debt: the First 5000 Years*
Friedrich Hayek's *The Road to Serfdom*
Karen Ho's *Liquidated: An Ethnography of Wall Street*

John Maynard Keynes's *The General Theory of Employment, Interest and Money*
Charles P. Kindleberger's *Manias, Panics and Crashes*
Robert Lucas's *Why Doesn't Capital Flow from Rich to Poor Countries?*
Burton G. Malkiel's *A Random Walk Down Wall Street*
Thomas Robert Malthus's *An Essay on the Principle of Population*
Karl Marx's *Capital*
Thomas Piketty's *Capital in the Twenty-First Century*
Amartya Sen's *Development as Freedom*
Adam Smith's *The Wealth of Nations*
Nassim Nicholas Taleb's *The Black Swan: The Impact of the Highly Improbable*
Amos Tversky's & Daniel Kahneman's *Judgment under Uncertainty: Heuristics and Biases*
Mahbub Ul Haq's *Reflections on Human Development*
Max Weber's *The Protestant Ethic and the Spirit of Capitalism*

FEMINISM AND GENDER STUDIES

Judith Butler's *Gender Trouble*
Simone De Beauvoir's *The Second Sex*
Michel Foucault's *History of Sexuality*
Betty Friedan's *The Feminine Mystique*
Saba Mahmood's *The Politics of Piety: The Islamic Revival and the Feminist Subject*
Joan Wallach Scott's *Gender and the Politics of History*
Mary Wollstonecraft's *A Vindication of the Rights of Woman*
Virginia Woolf's *A Room of One's Own*

GEOGRAPHY

The Brundtland Report's *Our Common Future*
Rachel Carson's *Silent Spring*
Charles Darwin's *On the Origin of Species*
James Ferguson's *The Anti-Politics Machine*
Jane Jacobs's *The Death and Life of Great American Cities*
James Lovelock's *Gaia: A New Look at Life on Earth*
Amartya Sen's *Development as Freedom*
Mathis Wackernagel & William Rees's *Our Ecological Footprint*

HISTORY

Janet Abu-Lughod's *Before European Hegemony*
Benedict Anderson's *Imagined Communities*
Bernard Bailyn's *The Ideological Origins of the American Revolution*
Hanna Batatu's *The Old Social Classes And The Revolutionary Movements Of Iraq*
Christopher Browning's *Ordinary Men: Reserve Police Batallion 101 and the Final Solution in Poland*
Edmund Burke's *Reflections on the Revolution in France*
William Cronon's *Nature's Metropolis: Chicago And The Great West*
Alfred W. Crosby's *The Columbian Exchange*
Hamid Dabashi's *Iran: A People Interrupted*
David Brion Davis's *The Problem of Slavery in the Age of Revolution*
Nathalie Zemon Davis's *The Return of Martin Guerre*
Jared Diamond's *Guns, Germs & Steel: the Fate of Human Societies*
Frank Dikotter's *Mao's Great Famine*
John W Dower's *War Without Mercy: Race And Power In The Pacific War*
W. E. B. Du Bois's *The Souls of Black Folk*
Richard J. Evans's *In Defence of History*
Lucien Febvre's *The Problem of Unbelief in the 16th Century*
Sheila Fitzpatrick's *Everyday Stalinism*

Eric Foner's *Reconstruction: America's Unfinished Revolution, 1863-1877*
Michel Foucault's *Discipline and Punish*
Michel Foucault's *History of Sexuality*
Francis Fukuyama's *The End of History and the Last Man*
John Lewis Gaddis's *We Now Know: Rethinking Cold War History*
Ernest Gellner's *Nations and Nationalism*
Eugene Genovese's *Roll, Jordan, Roll: The World the Slaves Made*
Carlo Ginzburg's *The Night Battles*
Daniel Goldhagen's *Hitler's Willing Executioners*
Jack Goldstone's *Revolution and Rebellion in the Early Modern World*
Antonio Gramsci's *The Prison Notebooks*
Alexander Hamilton, John Jay & James Madison's *The Federalist Papers*
Christopher Hill's *The World Turned Upside Down*
Carole Hillenbrand's *The Crusades: Islamic Perspectives*
Thomas Hobbes's *Leviathan*
Eric Hobsbawm's *The Age Of Revolution*
John A. Hobson's *Imperialism: A Study*
Albert Hourani's *History of the Arab Peoples*
Samuel P. Huntington's *The Clash of Civilizations and the Remaking of World Order*
C. L. R. James's *The Black Jacobins*
Tony Judt's *Postwar: A History of Europe Since 1945*
Ernst Kantorowicz's *The King's Two Bodies: A Study in Medieval Political Theology*
Paul Kennedy's *The Rise and Fall of the Great Powers*
Ian Kershaw's *The "Hitler Myth": Image and Reality in the Third Reich*
John Maynard Keynes's *The General Theory of Employment, Interest and Money*
Charles P. Kindleberger's *Manias, Panics and Crashes*
Martin Luther King Jr's *Why We Can't Wait*
Henry Kissinger's *World Order: Reflections on the Character of Nations and the Course of History*
Thomas Kuhn's *The Structure of Scientific Revolutions*
Georges Lefebvre's *The Coming of the French Revolution*
John Locke's *Two Treatises of Government*
Niccolò Machiavelli's *The Prince*
Thomas Robert Malthus's *An Essay on the Principle of Population*
Mahmood Mamdani's *Citizen and Subject: Contemporary Africa And The Legacy Of Late Colonialism*
Karl Marx's *Capital*
Stanley Milgram's *Obedience to Authority*
John Stuart Mill's *On Liberty*
Thomas Paine's *Common Sense*
Thomas Paine's *Rights of Man*
Geoffrey Parker's *Global Crisis: War, Climate Change and Catastrophe in the Seventeenth Century*
Jonathan Riley-Smith's *The First Crusade and the Idea of Crusading*
Jean-Jacques Rousseau's *The Social Contract*
Joan Wallach Scott's *Gender and the Politics of History*
Theda Skocpol's *States and Social Revolutions*
Adam Smith's *The Wealth of Nations*
Timothy Snyder's *Bloodlands: Europe Between Hitler and Stalin*
Sun Tzu's *The Art of War*
Keith Thomas's *Religion and the Decline of Magic*
Thucydides's *The History of the Peloponnesian War*
Frederick Jackson Turner's *The Significance of the Frontier in American History*
Odd Arne Westad's *The Global Cold War: Third World Interventions And The Making Of Our Times*

LITERATURE

Chinua Achebe's *An Image of Africa: Racism in Conrad's Heart of Darkness*
Roland Barthes's *Mythologies*
Homi K. Bhabha's *The Location of Culture*
Judith Butler's *Gender Trouble*
Simone De Beauvoir's *The Second Sex*
Ferdinand De Saussure's *Course in General Linguistics*
T. S. Eliot's *The Sacred Wood: Essays on Poetry and Criticism*
Zora Neale Huston's *Characteristics of Negro Expression*
Toni Morrison's *Playing in the Dark: Whiteness in the American Literary Imagination*
Edward Said's *Orientalism*
Gayatri Chakravorty Spivak's *Can the Subaltern Speak?*
Mary Wollstonecraft's *A Vindication of the Rights of Women*
Virginia Woolf's *A Room of One's Own*

PHILOSOPHY

Elizabeth Anscombe's *Modern Moral Philosophy*
Hannah Arendt's *The Human Condition*
Aristotle's *Metaphysics*
Aristotle's *Nicomachean Ethics*
Edmund Gettier's *Is Justified True Belief Knowledge?*
Georg Wilhelm Friedrich Hegel's *Phenomenology of Spirit*
David Hume's *Dialogues Concerning Natural Religion*
David Hume's *The Enquiry for Human Understanding*
Immanuel Kant's *Religion within the Boundaries of Mere Reason*
Immanuel Kant's *Critique of Pure Reason*
Søren Kierkegaard's *The Sickness Unto Death*
Søren Kierkegaard's *Fear and Trembling*
C. S. Lewis's *The Abolition of Man*
Alasdair MacIntyre's *After Virtue*
Marcus Aurelius's *Meditations*
Friedrich Nietzsche's *On the Genealogy of Morality*
Friedrich Nietzsche's *Beyond Good and Evil*
Plato's *Republic*
Plato's *Symposium*
Jean-Jacques Rousseau's *The Social Contract*
Gilbert Ryle's *The Concept of Mind*
Baruch Spinoza's *Ethics*
Sun Tzu's *The Art of War*
Ludwig Wittgenstein's *Philosophical Investigations*

POLITICS

Benedict Anderson's *Imagined Communities*
Aristotle's *Politics*
Bernard Bailyn's *The Ideological Origins of the American Revolution*
Edmund Burke's *Reflections on the Revolution in France*
John C. Calhoun's *A Disquisition on Government*
Ha-Joon Chang's *Kicking Away the Ladder*
Hamid Dabashi's *Iran: A People Interrupted*
Hamid Dabashi's *Theology of Discontent: The Ideological Foundation of the Islamic Revolution in Iran*
Robert Dahl's *Democracy and its Critics*
Robert Dahl's *Who Governs?*
David Brion Davis's *The Problem of Slavery in the Age of Revolution*

The Macat Library By Discipline

Alexis De Tocqueville's *Democracy in America*
James Ferguson's *The Anti-Politics Machine*
Frank Dikotter's *Mao's Great Famine*
Sheila Fitzpatrick's *Everyday Stalinism*
Eric Foner's *Reconstruction: America's Unfinished Revolution, 1863-1877*
Milton Friedman's *Capitalism and Freedom*
Francis Fukuyama's *The End of History and the Last Man*
John Lewis Gaddis's *We Now Know: Rethinking Cold War History*
Ernest Gellner's *Nations and Nationalism*
David Graeber's *Debt: the First 5000 Years*
Antonio Gramsci's *The Prison Notebooks*
Alexander Hamilton, John Jay & James Madison's *The Federalist Papers*
Friedrich Hayek's *The Road to Serfdom*
Christopher Hill's *The World Turned Upside Down*
Thomas Hobbes's *Leviathan*
John A. Hobson's *Imperialism: A Study*
Samuel P. Huntington's *The Clash of Civilizations and the Remaking of World Order*
Tony Judt's *Postwar: A History of Europe Since 1945*
David C. Kang's *China Rising: Peace, Power and Order in East Asia*
Paul Kennedy's *The Rise and Fall of Great Powers*
Robert Keohane's *After Hegemony*
Martin Luther King Jr.'s *Why We Can't Wait*
Henry Kissinger's *World Order: Reflections on the Character of Nations and the Course of History*
John Locke's *Two Treatises of Government*
Niccolò Machiavelli's *The Prince*
Thomas Robert Malthus's *An Essay on the Principle of Population*
Mahmood Mamdani's *Citizen and Subject: Contemporary Africa And The Legacy Of Late Colonialism*
Karl Marx's *Capital*
John Stuart Mill's *On Liberty*
John Stuart Mill's *Utilitarianism*
Hans Morgenthau's *Politics Among Nations*
Thomas Paine's *Common Sense*
Thomas Paine's *Rights of Man*
Thomas Piketty's *Capital in the Twenty-First Century*
Robert D. Putman's *Bowling Alone*
John Rawls's *Theory of Justice*
Jean-Jacques Rousseau's *The Social Contract*
Theda Skocpol's *States and Social Revolutions*
Adam Smith's *The Wealth of Nations*
Sun Tzu's *The Art of War*
Henry David Thoreau's *Civil Disobedience*
Thucydides's *The History of the Peloponnesian War*
Kenneth Waltz's *Theory of International Politics*
Max Weber's *Politics as a Vocation*
Odd Arne Westad's *The Global Cold War: Third World Interventions And The Making Of Our Times*

POSTCOLONIAL STUDIES

Roland Barthes's *Mythologies*
Frantz Fanon's *Black Skin, White Masks*
Homi K. Bhabha's *The Location of Culture*
Gustavo Gutiérrez's *A Theology of Liberation*
Edward Said's *Orientalism*
Gayatri Chakravorty Spivak's *Can the Subaltern Speak?*

PSYCHOLOGY

Gordon Allport's *The Nature of Prejudice*
Alan Baddeley & Graham Hitch's *Aggression: A Social Learning Analysis*
Albert Bandura's *Aggression: A Social Learning Analysis*
Leon Festinger's *A Theory of Cognitive Dissonance*
Sigmund Freud's *The Interpretation of Dreams*
Betty Friedan's *The Feminine Mystique*
Michael R. Gottfredson & Travis Hirschi's *A General Theory of Crime*
Eric Hoffer's *The True Believer: Thoughts on the Nature of Mass Movements*
William James's *Principles of Psychology*
Elizabeth Loftus's *Eyewitness Testimony*
A. H. Maslow's *A Theory of Human Motivation*
Stanley Milgram's *Obedience to Authority*
Steven Pinker's *The Better Angels of Our Nature*
Oliver Sacks's *The Man Who Mistook His Wife For a Hat*
Richard Thaler & Cass Sunstein's *Nudge: Improving Decisions About Health, Wealth and Happiness*
Amos Tversky's *Judgment under Uncertainty: Heuristics and Biases*
Philip Zimbardo's *The Lucifer Effect*

SCIENCE

Rachel Carson's *Silent Spring*
William Cronon's *Nature's Metropolis: Chicago And The Great West*
Alfred W. Crosby's *The Columbian Exchange*
Charles Darwin's *On the Origin of Species*
Richard Dawkin's *The Selfish Gene*
Thomas Kuhn's *The Structure of Scientific Revolutions*
Geoffrey Parker's *Global Crisis: War, Climate Change and Catastrophe in the Seventeenth Century*
Mathis Wackernagel & William Rees's *Our Ecological Footprint*

SOCIOLOGY

Michelle Alexander's *The New Jim Crow: Mass Incarceration in the Age of Colorblindness*
Gordon Allport's *The Nature of Prejudice*
Albert Bandura's *Aggression: A Social Learning Analysis*
Hanna Batatu's *The Old Social Classes And The Revolutionary Movements Of Iraq*
Ha-Joon Chang's *Kicking Away the Ladder*
W. E. B. Du Bois's *The Souls of Black Folk*
Émile Durkheim's *On Suicide*
Frantz Fanon's *Black Skin, White Masks*
Frantz Fanon's *The Wretched of the Earth*
Eric Foner's *Reconstruction: America's Unfinished Revolution, 1863-1877*
Eugene Genovese's *Roll, Jordan, Roll: The World the Slaves Made*
Jack Goldstone's *Revolution and Rebellion in the Early Modern World*
Antonio Gramsci's *The Prison Notebooks*
Richard Herrnstein & Charles A Murray's *The Bell Curve: Intelligence and Class Structure in American Life*
Eric Hoffer's *The True Believer: Thoughts on the Nature of Mass Movements*
Jane Jacobs's *The Death and Life of Great American Cities*
Robert Lucas's *Why Doesn't Capital Flow from Rich to Poor Countries?*
Jay Macleod's *Ain't No Makin' It: Aspirations and Attainment in a Low Income Neighborhood*
Elaine May's *Homeward Bound: American Families in the Cold War Era*
Douglas McGregor's *The Human Side of Enterprise*
C. Wright Mills's *The Sociological Imagination*

Thomas Piketty's *Capital in the Twenty-First Century*
Robert D. Putman's *Bowling Alone*
David Riesman's *The Lonely Crowd: A Study of the Changing American Character*
Edward Said's *Orientalism*
Joan Wallach Scott's *Gender and the Politics of History*
Theda Skocpol's *States and Social Revolutions*
Max Weber's *The Protestant Ethic and the Spirit of Capitalism*

THEOLOGY

Augustine's *Confessions*
Benedict's *Rule of St Benedict*
Gustavo Gutiérrez's *A Theology of Liberation*
Carole Hillenbrand's *The Crusades: Islamic Perspectives*
David Hume's *Dialogues Concerning Natural Religion*
Immanuel Kant's *Religion within the Boundaries of Mere Reason*
Ernst Kantorowicz's *The King's Two Bodies: A Study in Medieval Political Theology*
Søren Kierkegaard's *The Sickness Unto Death*
C. S. Lewis's *The Abolition of Man*
Saba Mahmood's *The Politics of Piety: The Islamic Revival and the Feminist Subje*ct
Baruch Spinoza's *Ethics*
Keith Thomas's *Religion and the Decline of Magic*

COMING SOON

Chris Argyris's *The Individual and the Organisation*
Seyla Benhabib's *The Rights of Others*
Walter Benjamin's *The Work Of Art in the Age of Mechanical Reproduction*
John Berger's *Ways of Seeing*
Pierre Bourdieu's *Outline of a Theory of Practice*
Mary Douglas's *Purity and Danger*
Roland Dworkin's *Taking Rights Seriously*
James G. March's *Exploration and Exploitation in Organisational Learning*
Ikujiro Nonaka's *A Dynamic Theory of Organizational Knowledge Creation*
Griselda Pollock's *Vision and Difference*
Amartya Sen's *Inequality Re-Examined*
Susan Sontag's *On Photography*
Yasser Tabbaa's *The Transformation of Islamic Art*
Ludwig von Mises's *Theory of Money and Credit*

Macat Disciplines

Access the greatest ideas and thinkers across entire disciplines, including

Postcolonial Studies

Roland Barthes's *Mythologies*
Frantz Fanon's *Black Skin, White Masks*
Homi K. Bhabha's *The Location of Culture*
Gustavo Gutiérrez's *A Theology of Liberation*
Edward Said's *Orientalism*
Gayatri Chakravorty Spivak's *Can the Subaltern Speak?*

Macat Disciplines

*Access the greatest ideas and thinkers
across entire disciplines, including*

AFRICANA STUDIES

Chinua Achebe's *An Image of Africa:
Racism in Conrad's Heart of Darkness*

W. E. B. Du Bois's *The Souls of Black Folk*

Zora Neale Hurston's *Characteristics of Negro Expression*

Martin Luther King Jr.'s *Why We Can't Wait*

Toni Morrison's *Playing in the Dark:
Whiteness in the American Literary Imagination*

Macat analyses are available from all good bookshops and libraries.

Access hundreds of analyses through one, multimedia tool.
Join free for one month **library.macat.com**

Macat Disciplines

Access the greatest ideas and thinkers across entire disciplines, including

FEMINISM, GENDER AND QUEER STUDIES

Simone De Beauvoir's
The Second Sex

Michel Foucault's
History of Sexuality

Betty Friedan's
The Feminine Mystique

Saba Mahmood's
*The Politics of Piety:
The Islamic Revival and
the Feminist Subject*

Joan Wallach Scott's
*Gender and the
Politics of History*

Mary Wollstonecraft's
*A Vindication of the
Rights of Woman*

Virginia Woolf's
A Room of One's Own

Judith Butler's
Gender Trouble

Macat analyses are available from all good bookshops and libraries.

Access hundreds of analyses through one, multimedia tool.
Join free for one month **library.macat.com**

Macat Disciplines

Access the greatest ideas and thinkers across entire disciplines, including

CRIMINOLOGY

Michelle Alexander's
The New Jim Crow: Mass Incarceration in the Age of Colorblindness

Michael R. Gottfredson & Travis Hirschi's
A General Theory of Crime

Elizabeth Loftus's
Eyewitness Testimony

Richard Herrnstein & Charles A. Murray's
The Bell Curve: Intelligence and Class Structure in American Life

Jay Macleod's
Ain't No Makin' It: Aspirations and Attainment in a Low-Income Neighborhood

Philip Zimbardo's
The Lucifer Effect

Macat Disciplines

Access the greatest ideas and thinkers across entire disciplines, including

INEQUALITY

Ha-Joon Chang's, *Kicking Away the Ladder*

David Graeber's, *Debt: The First 5000 Years*

Robert E. Lucas's, *Why Doesn't Capital Flow from Rich To Poor Countries?*

Thomas Piketty's, *Capital in the Twenty-First Century*

Amartya Sen's, *Inequality Re-Examined*

Mahbub Ul Haq's, *Reflections on Human Development*

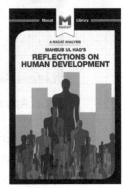

Macat Disciplines

Access the greatest ideas and thinkers across entire disciplines, including

MAN AND THE ENVIRONMENT

The Brundtland Report's, *Our Common Future*
Rachel Carson's, *Silent Spring*
James Lovelock's, *Gaia: A New Look at Life on Earth*
Mathis Wackernagel & William Rees's, *Our Ecological Footprint*

Macat analyses are available from all good bookshops and libraries.

Access hundreds of analyses through one, multimedia tool.
Join free for one month **library.macat.com**

Macat Disciplines

Access the greatest ideas and thinkers across entire disciplines, including

THE FUTURE OF DEMOCRACY

Robert A. Dahl's, *Democracy and Its Critics*
Robert A. Dahl's, *Who Governs?*
Alexis De Toqueville's, *Democracy in America*
Niccolò Machiavelli's, *The Prince*
John Stuart Mill's, *On Liberty*
Robert D. Putnam's, *Bowling Alone*
Jean-Jacques Rousseau's, *The Social Contract*
Henry David Thoreau's, *Civil Disobedience*

Macat Pairs

Analyse historical and modern issues from opposite sides of an argument. Pairs include:

RACE AND IDENTITY

Zora Neale Hurston's
Characteristics of Negro Expression

Using material collected on anthropological expeditions to the South, Zora Neale Hurston explains how expression in African American culture in the early twentieth century departs from the art of white America. At the time, African American art was often criticized for copying white culture. For Hurston, this criticism misunderstood how art works. European tradition views art as something fixed. But Hurston describes a creative process that is alive, ever-changing, and largely improvisational. She maintains that African American art works through a process called 'mimicry'—where an imitated object or verbal pattern, for example, is reshaped and altered until it becomes something new, novel—and worthy of attention.

Frantz Fanon's
Black Skin, White Masks

Black Skin, White Masks offers a radical analysis of the psychological effects of colonization on the colonized.

Fanon witnessed the effects of colonization first hand both in his birthplace, Martinique, and again later in life when he worked as a psychiatrist in another French colony, Algeria. His text is uncompromising in form and argument. He dissects the dehumanizing effects of colonialism, arguing that it destroys the native sense of identity, forcing people to adapt to an alien set of values—including a core belief that they are inferior. This results in deep psychological trauma.

Fanon's work played a pivotal role in the civil rights movements of the 1960s.

Macat analyses are available from all good bookshops and libraries.

Access hundreds of analyses through one, multimedia tool.
Join free for one month **library.macat.com**

Macat Pairs

Analyse historical and modern issues from opposite sides of an argument. Pairs include:

INTERNATIONAL RELATIONS IN THE 21ST CENTURY

Samuel P. Huntington's
The Clash of Civilisations

In his highly influential 1996 book, Huntington offers a vision of a post-Cold War world in which conflict takes place not between competing ideologies but between cultures. The worst clash, he argues, will be between the Islamic world and the West: the West's arrogance and belief that its culture is a "gift" to the world will come into conflict with Islam's obstinacy and concern that its culture is under attack from a morally decadent "other."

Clash inspired much debate between different political schools of thought. But its greatest impact came in helping define American foreign policy in the wake of the 2001 terrorist attacks in New York and Washington.

Francis Fukuyama's
The End of History and the Last Man

Published in 1992, *The End of History and the Last Man* argues that capitalist democracy is the final destination for all societies. Fukuyama believed democracy triumphed during the Cold War because it lacks the "fundamental contradictions" inherent in communism and satisfies our yearning for freedom and equality. Democracy therefore marks the endpoint in the evolution of ideology, and so the "end of history." There will still be "events," but no fundamental change in ideology.

Macat Pairs

Analyse historical and modern issues from opposite sides of an argument. Pairs include:

HOW TO RUN AN ECONOMY

John Maynard Keynes's
The General Theory OF Employment, Interest and Money

Classical economics suggests that market economies are self-correcting in times of recession or depression, and tend toward full employment and output. But English economist John Maynard Keynes disagrees.

In his ground-breaking 1936 study *The General Theory*, Keynes argues that traditional economics has misunderstood the causes of unemployment. Employment is not determined by the price of labor; it is directly linked to demand. Keynes believes market economies are by nature unstable, and so require government intervention. Spurred on by the social catastrophe of the Great Depression of the 1930s, he sets out to revolutionize the way the world thinks

Milton Friedman's
The Role of Monetary Policy

Friedman's 1968 paper changed the course of economic theory. In just 17 pages, he demolished existing theory and outlined an effective alternate monetary policy designed to secure 'high employment, stable prices and rapid growth.'

Friedman demonstrated that monetary policy plays a vital role in broader economic stability and argued that economists got their monetary policy wrong in the 1950s and 1960s by misunderstanding the relationship between inflation and unemployment. Previous generations of economists had believed that governments could permanently decrease unemployment by permitting inflation—and vice versa. Friedman's most original contribution was to show that this supposed trade-off is an illusion that only works in the short term.

Macat Pairs

Analyse historical and modern issues from opposite sides of an argument. Pairs include:

ARE WE FUNDAMENTALLY GOOD - OR BAD?

Steven Pinker's
The Better Angels of Our Nature

Stephen Pinker's gloriously optimistic 2011 book argues that, despite humanity's biological tendency toward violence, we are, in fact, less violent today than ever before. To prove his case, Pinker lays out pages of detailed statistical evidence. For him, much of the credit for the decline goes to the eighteenth-century Enlightenment movement, whose ideas of liberty, tolerance, and respect for the value of human life filtered down through society and affected how people thought. That psychological change led to behavioral change—and overall we became more peaceful. Critics countered that humanity could never overcome the biological urge toward violence; others argued that Pinker's statistics were flawed.

Philip Zimbardo's
The Lucifer Effect

Some psychologists believe those who commit cruelty are innately evil. Zimbardo disagrees. In *The Lucifer Effect*, he argues that sometimes good people do evil things simply because of the situations they find themselves in, citing many historical examples to illustrate his point. Zimbardo details his 1971 Stanford prison experiment, where ordinary volunteers playing guards in a mock prison rapidly became abusive. But he also describes the tortures committed by US army personnel in Iraq's Abu Ghraib prison in 2003—and how he himself testified in defence of one of those guards. committed by US army personnel in Iraq's Abu Ghraib prison in 2003—and how he himself testified in defence of one of those guards.

Macat analyses are available from all good bookshops and libraries.

Access hundreds of analyses through one, multimedia tool.
Join free for one month **library.macat.com**

Macat Pairs

Analyse historical and modern issues from opposite sides of an argument. Pairs include:

HOW WE RELATE TO EACH OTHER AND SOCIETY

Jean-Jacques Rousseau's
The Social Contract

Rousseau's famous work sets out the radical concept of the 'social contract': a give-and-take relationship between individual freedom and social order.

If people are free to do as they like, governed only by their own sense of justice, they are also vulnerable to chaos and violence. To avoid this, Rousseau proposes, they should agree to give up some freedom to benefit from the protection of social and political organization. But this deal is only just if societies are led by the collective needs and desires of the people, and able to control the private interests of individuals. For Rousseau, the only legitimate form of government is rule by the people.

Robert D. Putnam's
Bowling Alone

In *Bowling Alone*, Robert Putnam argues that Americans have become disconnected from one another and from the institutions of their common life, and investigates the consequences of this change.

Looking at a range of indicators, from membership in formal organizations to the number of invitations being extended to informal dinner parties, Putnam demonstrates that Americans are interacting less and creating less "social capital" – with potentially disastrous implications for their society.

It would be difficult to overstate the impact of *Bowling Alone*, one of the most frequently cited social science publications of the last half-century.

Macat analyses are available from all good bookshops and libraries.

Access hundreds of analyses through one, multimedia tool.
Join free for one month **library.macat.com**